in_**focus**

Healthy Lives
for Vulnerable Women and Children

in_**focus**

IDRC's *in_focus* collection tackles current and pressing issues in sustainable international development. Each publication distills IDRC's research experience with an eye to drawing out important lessons, observations, and recommendations. Each also serves as a focal point for an IDRC website page that probes the issue more deeply, and is constructed to serve the differing information needs of IDRC's various readers. Each *in_focus* book may be browsed online at **www.idrc.ca**.

IDRC welcomes any feedback on this publication. Please direct your comments to the publisher at **info@idrc.ca**.

in_focus

Healthy Lives
for Vulnerable Women and Children

APPLYING HEALTH SYSTEMS RESEARCH

Sue Godt, Irene Agyepong,
Walter Flores, and Gita Sen

INTERNATIONAL DEVELOPMENT RESEARCH CENTRE
Ottawa • Cairo • Montevideo • Nairobi • New Delhi

Published by the International Development Research Centre
PO Box 8500, Ottawa, ON, Canada K1G 3H9
www.idrc.ca / info@idrc.ca

The research presented in this publication was carried out with the aid of a
grant from the International Development Research Centre (IDRC), Ottawa,
Canada. The views expressed herein do not necessarily represent those of
IDRC or its Board of Governors.

ISBN 978-1-55250-601-1
ISBN (ebook) 978-1-55250-604-2

This publication may be read online at www.idrc.ca, and serves as the focal
point for a thematic website: **www.idrc.ca/healthy-lives**.

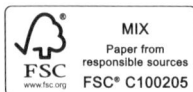

Contents

Part 3. Using health systems research to build healthy lives ➤ 27

Evidence from select national, regional, and global examples shows the background, thinking, approaches, and main findings that can help us address identified challenges and build better health systems.

Part 4. Lessons learned and looking forward ➤ 69

Lessons related to six specific enveloping topics have been gleaned from this research. They can assist in improving equity, governance, and health systems, providing improved outcomes for vulnerable groups.

Executive Summary

The issue

The Sustainable Development Goals (SDGs) aim to create healthy lives and promote the well-being of all. There are challenges to ensuring that the most vulnerable populations, including women, children, and adolescents, are able to enjoy these outcomes. Much of their poor health is caused by poverty, gender, lack of education, and social marginalization as well as inaccessible healthcare services. Strong, equitable, and well-governed health systems can contribute to sustainably improving their lives. Such health systems – not health services – engage multisectorally with stakeholders to address the underlying causes of poor health and build quality, accessible, and affordable primary healthcare services.

But building strong health systems is challenging. Key barriers include poor data and weak health information systems; under-resourced, fragmented, and inaccessible healthcare services; political commitment to address the underlying causes of poor health; and lack of governance and accountability to ensure appropriate policy development with sufficient resource allocation to enable effective sustainable implementation.

The research

This book draws on 15 years of IDRC-funded health systems research undertaken by researchers working closely with communities and decision-makers. They have generated contextually relevant evidence at local, national, regional, and global levels to tackle these entrenched health systems challenges.

The quality of data collection and health information systems can be sustainably strengthened by undertaking health systems research with relevant health structures. In India, new national guidelines for maternal death reviews were introduced based on evidence demonstrating that existing reviews obscured the systemic neglect of women's health needs in pregnancy and childbirth and the tendency of health professionals to mask their own failures. Two Nigerian state governments institutionalized evidence-based decision-making by establishing innovative real-time community surveillance systems through which health workers visited every household and transmitted 'live' data to the ministry planning departments. These two examples 'counted' vulnerable women who were often invisible to the system and facilitated planning that responded to their health needs. Importantly, the data was taken back in appropriate formats to those responsible for driving change: facility performance scorecards for health planners, improved diagnostic tools, and engagement platforms for health workers, docudramas, and discussion groups for communities.

Health systems researchers advanced efforts to implement the ambitious SDG goal around Universal Health Coverage (UHC). Their evidence documented the long-term impoverishing impact of health fees on poor households as well as the challenges confronting governments trying to mitigate the suffering by applying partial and fragmented subsidies. Researchers have developed relevant analytical tools and guides to support governments in planning UHC implementation. Evidence is showing how putting vulnerable women and adolescents at the centre of UHC processes can strengthen the overall system. Significantly, the research has demonstrated that UHC is not a technical issue; adopting UHC is a political decision requiring social solidarity about the value of providing care to vulnerable populations.

Ultimately, accountability, governance, and stewardship of health resources are needed to ensure strategic and consistent decision-making and resource allocation to build strong health systems. The evidence has shown that this governance is needed – and makes a difference – from local to national to global levels. Health systems researchers and stakeholders in Guatemala and Uganda for example worked with vulnerable communities to monitor and report on quality of service delivery and to negotiate improvements to maternal health facilities. In East, Central, and Southern Africa, researchers worked with authorities to strengthen governance at scale, both nationally and regionally. Their research also documented systemic global factors negatively influencing efforts to improve health services, including reproductive, maternal, and child health services. Strategically, they also identified opportunities for South-South collaboration to address these global-level factors.

To ensure that evidence is used to drive change, researchers are building relationships of trust and respect with decision-makers, practitioners, and communities as well as creating platforms of engagement that facilitate frank debate and deepened discourse around the evidence in ways that have influenced policy and practice at local, national, and global levels.

The lessons

We have distilled six lessons from the research and experience to inform and inspire a new generation of health leaders and researchers, while sharing with others in the global health community, including funding organizations, some critical reflections on the remaining challenges.

Development matters – For sustainable improvement in health outcomes, it is necessary to address the root causes of poor health including factors such as gender, poverty, lack of education, and social marginalization. Otherwise we will always be dealing with the symptoms of poor health. Finding sustainable solutions that address root causes in vulnerable communities and in dysfunctional systems takes time because change is a cumulative process and not achieved through a series of siloed, one-off interventions.

People matter – Improving health outcomes cannot happen without the full engagement of all who can contribute to change. Vulnerable populations, especially disadvantaged women, children, and adolescents need to be put at the centre of health planning. Community members, particularly the vulnerable, need to be active engaged citizens; health providers need the required support to fully provide quality services; and decision-makers need information, authority, and resources to make informed programmatic and resource-allocation decisions.

Politics matter – Recognizing that the political nature of health shapes solutions that address the underlying inequities, IDRC-funded researchers have demonstrated how to work from community to global levels to address the issues of politics and power that impede equitable health systems.

Systems matter – Health systems must be understood and addressed as a whole. Prioritizing individual components (human resources, health information), individual services (immunization), individual diseases (HIV), or individual groups (mothers and children) in isolation will further fragment efforts.

Evidence matters – Rigorous methodologies are needed to generate reliable data and evidence to inform changes in practice and policy. Of greatest importance are methodologies that analyze exclusion and equity, and which can generate actionable findings. If research is not driven by the needs of communities and stakeholders seeking to inform themselves and drive change, it is unlikely to be relevant.

Funding matters – Low- and middle-income countries (LMICs) are increasingly mobilizing their own resources to implement UHC as a mechanism for providing quality affordable care to vulnerable populations. However, research has confirmed the continuing influence of donor agendas and priorities on national strategies and resource allocation decisions. Emerging reflections and lessons point to the need to put LMIC stakeholders and researchers, and their knowledge, at the centre of research and development processes so they can lead the research and use the findings to promote sustainable change. Funders can enable the space for LMIC stakeholder visioning and relationship-building rather than forcing prescriptive approaches and subsequently trying to ensure buy-in. Long-term funding windows of support, along with metrics of success that measure the important intermediate steps to ultimate change, are also needed.

Foreword

For researchers and stakeholders supported by the International Development Research Centre (IDRC) over the past 15 years, health research is not theoretical. It is about life and death issues affecting them, their families, and their communities. The stakeholders are dedicated, visionary, and never give up hope, despite daunting challenges in undertaking research and in encouraging its use in shaping policy and practice.

This *in_focus* title celebrates just a few of these amazing health system thought leaders funded by IDRC. Their experiences, their approaches, their results, and their successes are profiled in this book because they exemplify the effort that it takes to improve the health of the several billion marginalized people in the world today. It has been a privilege and an honour to build partnerships with this group of researchers and stakeholders. At IDRC, we remain inspired by their commitment and by the wealth and quality of expertise, experience, knowledge, and evidence that has been and continues to be developed.

It is with great pride that we co-author this edition with three distinguished thought leaders: Dr. Irene Agyepong from Ghana, Dr. Walter Flores from Guatemala, and Dr. Gita Sen from India.

Their voices are reflected in the book itself. Given their significant roles as global leaders who are putting issues of vulnerable communities on the public policy table, building the evidence base, and catalyzing stakeholder engagement to build strong equitable health systems, they have added immensely to this book.

Many thanks to Mary O'Neill for her background work on the book and to Nola Haddadian for her infinite patience in shepherding us through the process. Much gratitude to Juliana N. Gnamon and Juan Carlos Rivillas-Garcia for reviewing the French and Spanish texts, respectively. Heartfelt appreciation to team colleagues for enabling our joint learning and to Montasser Kamal for leading us forward and building on this foundation. There is deep recognition that the past 15 years have been a collective journey of action and reflection galvanized by the leadership, vision, and passion of Christina Zarowsky, Pat Naidoo, and Sharmila Mhatre. With particular gratitude to Sharmila for her invaluable and inspired insights during the conception and writing phases.

Sue Godt
International Development Research Centre

Preface

Setting the scene

We want to set the scene by sharing reflections on two health challenges that are confronting decision-makers at national and global levels.

Health emergencies: what Ebola taught us

The 2014 Ebola virus disease outbreak in West Africa's Guinea, Liberia, and Sierra Leone provided a wake-up call about our global interdependence. No country was immune as cases spread to Mali, Nigeria, Senegal, the United Kingdom, and the United States. There has since been growing acknowledgement that our individual and collective health security is inextricably tied together (Heymann et al. 2015; Gostin and Friedman 2015).

Important lessons were learned. First, the outbreak revealed **the systemic inequities within and across countries**. In affected parts of West Africa, local health services and surveillance systems were weak or missing, especially in rural and disadvantaged communities, resulting in "28,600 diagnosed cases and 11,000 deaths during the outbreak" (Green 2016: 2463). Other health services were curtailed as people avoided health facilities. Many facilities closed their doors as available resources were directed to Ebola prevention and treatment. During the outbreak, "more deaths probably ensued from other causes than from Ebola" (Gostin and Friedman 2015: 1903). Wilkinson and Leach (2014: 136) point to societal inequities in the regional history and the global economy that exacerbated the severity of the outbreak. Internationally, the more than US$ 4 billion commitment by funders was 15 times the combined annual national health budgets of the three countries. The amount also represented almost three times the annual cost of building universal health services that would have met all of the health needs in Guinea, Liberia, and Sierra Leone (Save the Children 2015).

Secondly, the outbreak demonstrated the **need to strengthen governance and accountability from community to global levels**. Internally, there was frequent mistrust of government and public health services by communities (Save the Children 2015; Wurie 2014; Kucharski and Piot 2014; Gostin and Friedman 2015; Wigmore 2015). The three affected governments themselves did not meet their obligations for emergency preparedness outlined in the International Health Regulations[1] (IHRs), which legally bind 196 countries to prevent and respond to acute public health risks. Likewise, international funders did not meet their obligations to supplement or build the capacity of the low-income affected countries, enabling them to meet their responsibilities. Many governments disregarded the IHRs by sealing off the three countries. Airlines stopped landing and governments refused entry to people arriving from Guinea, Liberia, and Sierra Leone.

Finally, as noted by Bill Gates and numerous others (Loewenson et al. 2015; Save the Children 2015; Barbiero 2014; Kieny et al. 2014; Heymann et al. 2015; Gostin and Friedman 2015),

> *there is a critical need* **to reinforce basic public health systems**, *including primary healthcare facilities, laboratories,*

surveillance systems and critical care facilities [...] Without a functioning health system, it is very hard for a country to end the cycle of disease and poverty. Health is so fundamental to development that even if there were no chance of another epidemic, building and improving health systems would be a worthwhile – and lifesaving – investment. [emphasis added] (Gates 2015: 1382)

Ensuring that women, children, and adolescents are not left behind

The ground-breaking 1994 International Conference on Population and Development[2] and its transformative Programme of Action[3] (United Nations Population Fund 2004) offered a powerful new vision of how to address the health problems of vulnerable women, children, and adolescents. Many health stakeholders at the time focused on a very narrow interpretation of maternal health and prioritized a package of interventions to promote safe deliveries (Rosenfield and Maine 1985; Maine and Rosenfield 1999). Population and development stakeholders focused narrowly on population control.

By 1994, a powerful women's health movement comprising researchers, civil society members, and government officials campaigned for a much broader approach encompassing sexual and reproductive health and rights (SRHR). The evidence was presented in an influential publication *Population Policies Reconsidered: Health, Empowerment, and Rights* edited by Gita Sen, Adrienne Germaine, and Lincoln Chen (1994) which argued that public policies should aim to "assure the rights and well-being of people, rather than simply attempting to limit the ultimate size of the world's population." They put the issues of gender and women's and girls' rights at the centre of the health and development process.

Tremendous challenges remain in achieving this vision. In 2014, Canada's International Development Research Centre (IDRC) funded a special journal supplement, led by Gita Sen, Adrienne Germain, and others to examine LMIC progress towards achieving the ambitious agenda over the previous 20 years and to reflect on challenges and opportunities for moving forward.

Contributors concluded that progress had been made towards improving SRHR outcomes and policies for service provision. But three major gaps remain: **inequitable access** to sexual and reproductive health (SRH) services, education and information, particularly for poor, rural women and adolescents; **substandard quality** of SRH services; and **non-existent or ineffective accountability** mechanisms to track progress and address inequalities and poor service quality (Germain et al. 2015: 139).

Sen and Govender (2015) argued against dealing with adolescents' and women's health needs in silos and advocated for centrally positioning them in health systems. **Overall system improvements and services benefitting everyone should be accompanied by "special attention to those whose needs are great and who are likely to fall behind"** [emphasis added] (Sen and Govender 2015: 235). They also advocated for multisectoral engagement to address the underlying causes of poor health, including early forced marriages and violence against women and girls.

Meeting the challenge

These examples reflect the growing consensus about the importance of developing strong, accountable health systems to sustainably meet the needs of vulnerable groups, and to prevent and better manage unexpected health emergencies. Both examples have underlined the importance of equitable access, quality services, and governance and accountability to promote sustainability.

But how can governments and stakeholders build these equitable sustainable health systems to achieve improved health outcomes? This issue of *in_focus* hopes to contribute to the discussion around this fundamental question.

IDRC has grappled with the issues of equity, governance, and health systems since 2002. Throughout the Millennium Development Goal (MDG)[4] era and the period of defining the new Sustainable Development Goals (SDGs),[5] it has worked with a remarkable group of researchers and stakeholders to seek sustainable ways of improving the health of the most vulnerable members of society. Given that women, children, and adolescents have consistently emerged as amongst the most marginalized, IDRC's health systems research support has increasingly focused on how systems can strengthen maternal and child health outcomes and address SRH needs. The Centre recognizes that if communities and countries can overcome the particular challenges to improving vulnerable women's, children's, and adolescents' health, then health for everyone will improve.

Improving the health of this vulnerable group, however, remains a challenge. At the end of the day, science and evidence tell us that it is not enough to simply count the deaths, deliver emergency relief during catastrophic moments, or to provide commodities such as oxytocin, antibiotics or magnesium sulphate (Horton 2014). What is needed is the stewardship, capacities, and fiscal space to ensure the existence of a system that offers a continuum of care and support for the adolescent and for the mother and her family. The system needs to be grounded in the context of a social, political, and cultural environment that demonstrates that women, children, and adolescents are valued. By addressing the root causes and social determinants of health, which is part of building strong health systems, benefits will accrue beyond these vulnerable groups to the wider community and to the national and social systems of which they are a part. In turn, these foundations will help to prevent, and quickly control, health emergencies such as the devastating 2014 Ebola outbreak in West Africa.

This book presents evidence generated over 15 years of health systems research supported by IDRC on how to improve equity, governance, and health systems and how to make the systems work for vulnerable groups. Readers will not find a blueprint or one-size-fits-all solution for addressing women's, children's, and adolescents' health challenges. There is no magic pill for sustainably improving the health of the most vulnerable members of our societies. Instead, this book attempts to distill lessons from research and experience supported across the globe so that it may inform and inspire a new generation of health leaders and researchers. It also aims to share with others in the global health community, including funding organizations, some critical reflections on the challenges that remain. The goal of this publication is thus to identify and link these lessons to reflections about the way forward to improve the lives of women, children, and adolescents and all vulnerable groups through improving equity, governance, and health systems.

Part 1 summarizes key issues that undermine efforts to improve health outcomes: the challenge of making vulnerable populations visible in the data; weak and ineffective health information systems; widespread inequities; poor governance and fragmentation of health systems; shifting donor priorities that have tended to focus on individual illnesses rather than underlying causes and system weaknesses; and a lack of UHC.

In Part 2, IDRC's approach to supporting research and fostering the use of evidence in health policy and practice is outlined in more detail. The section also explains the underlying principles that have guided the Centre's work: to help identify those who are uncounted; to understand the root causes of their health problems; and to support relevant stakeholders in developing sustainable solutions that strengthen the health delivery systems and accountability at all levels.

Part 3 presents the evidence and introduces the researchers, decision-makers, community members, and other stakeholders who have created this story. We have tried to pull out key reflections on the thinking that guided the research, on the approaches used, on the findings, and on the key challenges and opportunities. While only a handful of examples can be discussed in this short book, we have tried to include links and references in the e-book version[6] to the wealth of evidence and learning that has been generated over the years. In this way, we hope to provide a useful reference section for those who want to dig more deeply into the research.

The journey to healthy lives and well-being is not over. Tremendous challenges remain. Part 4 synthesizes the key lessons and broader issues that have emerged through IDRC's efforts over 15 years while Part 5 identifies gaps and strategic opportunities for the way forward.

Part 1

The issues and the development context

Global gains and persistent gaps in reproductive, maternal, and child health: what does the data tell us?

Maternal mortality in Uganda – putting the evidence on the table

The world took note when a group of young Ugandan lawyers stood in the Constitutional Court and filed a lawsuit about two women who had died in childbirth. The Ugandan non-profit Center for Health, Human Rights and Development,[7] a research organization supported by IDRC and headed by Moses Mulumba, represented a coalition of lawyers and organizations working to improve maternal health. The lawsuit contends that the Ugandan Government breached the women's human and constitutional rights by failing to provide them with basic maternal care. (CEHURD 2011; Dugger 2011; Wilson 2015)

The Facts

In rural Uganda, a woman in labour arrived at a local government health centre, just a few miles from her home. Sylvia Nalubowa was nearly 40 years old, in her seventh pregnancy, and though she did not know it, she was carrying twins. As required, she brought with her a pair of gloves, a plastic

continued...

sheet, sterile gauze, and other basic items that make up the "birthing kit" that all expectant mothers had to provide for their baby's delivery.

Her first child was born at the health centre, but as it became clear she was to deliver a second, and her labour grew difficult, the woman was referred to a district hospital 12 miles away. Her mother-in-law paid what money she had to cover the cost of transport. But upon arrival, a nurse demanded yet another payment before she would call a doctor to attend.

Despite her pleas, and offers to sell part of her land, a goat, or a pig so that she could pay later, the mother gradually bled to death that night, still waiting for help. Her unborn child died in her womb.

The court case also referred to Jennifer Anguko, an elected government official, who bled to death in labour in 2010. She died in a hospital that had only one midwife on duty and routinely lacked basic supplies such as sutures, despite serving as the emergency obstetric care centre for a region of almost three million people.

These cases are far from unique. In 2015, an estimated 830 women died every day in childbirth around the world. The deaths were largely preventable and the majority took place in low- and middle-income countries (LMICs) (World Health Organization [WHO] 2016b). Hemorrhages and other preventable conditions remain the leading proximate (or immediate direct) causes of mortality (Say et al. 2014). But as the needless deaths of Sylvia Nalubowa and Jennifer Anguko in Uganda show, health system failures, combined with social and contextual factors such as poverty and a lack of respect for women's rights, contribute significantly to the distal (or underlying) causes of mortality.

The health of women and children has long been a central preoccupation for governments and the international development community. Objectives for reducing child mortality and improving maternal health were core to the Millennium Development Goals[8] (MDGs) agreed to by UN member states in 2001. While progress toward these objectives fell short of targets,[9] significant gains were made as illustrated in Table 1.

Table 1. Changes in global mortality, 1990-2015			
Indicator	Global Percentage Decline 1990-2015	Rate (1990)	Rate (2015)
Infant mortality rate (deaths per thousand live births)	Almost 50%	63	32
Under five mortality rate (U5MR) (deaths per thousand live births)	53%	91	43
Maternal mortality ratio (MMR) (deaths per 100,000 live births)	53%	385	216

Sources: WHO et al. 2015; WHO Global Health Observatory [Data accessed March 14, 2017]

The SDGs[10] will now drive global priorities to 2030. Concerns about maternal and child health have been integrated into a broader, more comprehensive 'life-course' approach addressing the needs of women, children, and adolescents. National and global stakeholders are mobilizing around *The global strategy for women's, children's and adolescents' health (2016-2030): Survive, Thrive, Transform.*[11] The new target aims to reduce the global maternal mortality ratio (MMR) to less than 70 per 100,000 live births; to reduce neonatal mortality to at most 12 per 1,000 live births; and under-5 mortality to at most 25 per 1,000 live births. SDG 3[12] also aims to ensure universal access to sexual and reproductive healthcare services. Importantly, the Global Strategy emphasizes the creation of an enabling environment for health that will "transform societies so that women, children and adolescents everywhere can realize their rights to the highest attainable standards of health and well-being" which "in turn, will deliver enormous social, demographic and economic benefits."

Figure 1. Maternal mortality ratio (per 100,000 live births) by country and region, 2015

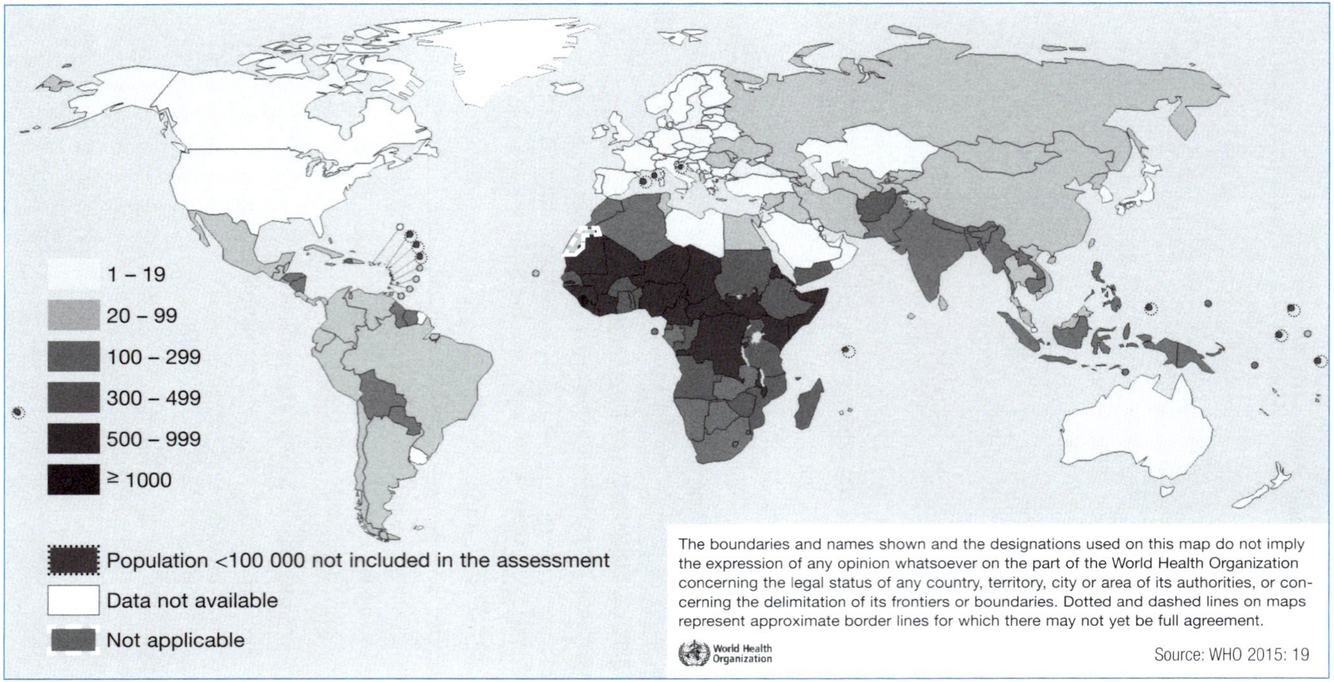

1 – 19
20 – 99
100 – 299
300 – 499
500 – 999
≥ 1000
Population <100 000 not included in the assessment
Data not available
Not applicable
The boundaries and names shown and the designations used on this map do not imply the expression of any opinion whatsoever on the part of the World Health Organization concerning the legal status of any country, territory, city or area of its authorities, or concerning the delimitation of its frontiers or boundaries. Dotted and dashed lines on maps represent approximate border lines for which there may not yet be full agreement.
World Health Organization

Source: WHO 2015: 19

Invisible vulnerable populations

These global-level statistics, however, do not reveal the whole picture. Figure 1 reflects the considerable gaps in progress to reduce maternal mortality within and across regions. The greatest progress since 1990 has been in East Asia, where the MMR declined by 72% in contrast to South Asia where almost 22% of global maternal deaths took place. Of great concern is the data showing that fully two-thirds of all maternal deaths occurred in sub-Saharan Africa (SSA) (WHO 2015: xi) despite this region having just over 13% of the total world population.[13]

Additional data is needed to help describe the challenges confronting SSA in reducing maternal mortality. This data has not been easy to collect and the WHO (2015: 26) noted that many of the most vulnerable populations are not even represented in the current global data. This gap can have devastating consequences because data that deepens understanding about specific conditions and population groups enables more specific and targeted policymaking, programming, and resource allocation. Gaps, however, are slowly being addressed as revealed in the following examples on HIV/AIDS and adolescent pregnancy.

Highlighting HIV/AIDS

Solid evidence now demonstrates that HIV/AIDS is a significant indirect cause of maternal death. For example, Kenya continues to experience a very high MMR with 510 women dying for every 100,000 live births (WHO et al. 2015: xi). Desai et al. (2013: 9), however, analyzed surveillance data over a five-year period from Western Kenya and concluded that two-thirds of pregnancy-related deaths were due to non-obstetric causes – 30% of the deaths were attributable to HIV/AIDS.

The WHO report on global trends in maternal mortality (WHO et al. 2015: 26) similarly noted that 7 of the 26 countries deemed as having made 'no progress' in reducing maternal mortality were affected by the HIV epidemic. Even though antiretroviral medica-

Table 2. Maternal mortality ratios and percentage of AIDS-related maternal deaths in selected countries of Southern Africa[14]		
Country	Maternal Mortality Ratio (MMR), 2015	AIDS-related indirect maternal deaths
Botswana	129	18%
South Africa	138	32.1%
Swaziland	389	18.6%

Source: WHO 2015: 51-55[15]

tions have helped reduce maternal mortality, tremendous challenges remain in further reducing mortality rates given the strain the epidemic continues to place on health systems and their infrastructure.

Highlighting adolescent pregnancy

Until recently, adolescent pregnancy was not well understood or reflected in the data and currently there is still limited data on the particularly vulnerable 10 to 14 year-old group. Adolescent pregnancy, however, is now solidly on the global agenda because it is recognized that early pregnancy undermines development goals and has a direct impact on efforts to reduce maternal and child mortality. Every year, some 16 million adolescent girls give birth, representing 11% of all births worldwide (WHO 2016a). These young mothers are at high risk of dying in delivery or developing an obstetric fistula, which can result in lifelong complications including incontinence, infertility, and social exclusion. Adolescent mothers are more likely to have more children and at shorter intervals. The rate of still births and deaths in the first weeks of life is 50% higher amongst babies born to teenage mothers. Sexual and reproductive health needs are largely unmet resulting in approximately three million unsafe abortions annually among girls aged 15 to 19 (WHO 2016a).

Looking at adolescent pregnancy in Niger demonstrates the need for data broken into even smaller units (i.e., disaggregated) in order to develop a more complete understanding of the issue. The country has recorded the highest rate of adolescent pregnancy in the world, with 51% of women aged 20 to 24 having had a live birth before the age of 18 (Loaiza and Liang 2013: 14). The national level data, however, obscures what happens at local and district levels where the responsibility for most health service delivery is located. Extreme disparities in health outcomes can be masked; for example, adolescents living in the region of Zinder in Niger are more than three times as likely to give birth before age 18 (68%) than their counterparts in the capital city Niamey (21%) (Loaiza and Liang 2013: 19). The disaggregated data points to the need for context-specific rather than generalized policies and programs.

There is also growing recognition of the valuable role that data can play to help explain the causes of early pregnancy, which are rooted in structural and social inequalities, including forced early marriage, gender-based violence, poverty, and low education levels. For example, the International Center for Research on Women (2016a) confirms that one-third of girls in LMICs are married before the age of 18. Poverty is a key factor and girls living in poor households are almost twice as likely to marry before 18 as girls in higher income households. Violence threatens the health of young women: globally, 29% of women aged 15 to 19 who have had sexual partners have experienced intimate partner violence (Woog et al. 2015) while the 2014 Global Summit to End Sexual Violence in Conflict has documented systemic sexual violence in conflict and fragile settings. Evidence demonstrates the link between high adolescent fertility rates and low levels of education; even girls in school are frequently forced to drop out once pregnant and this jeopardizes future economic prospects (Loaiza and Liang 2013). Access to sexual reproductive health services and supplies is lacking, which contributes to HIV being one of the leading causes of death globally for girls aged 10 to 19 and to pregnancy and child delivery complications being another major cause of adolescent mortality (International Center for Research on Women 2016b).

The need for better data and stronger health information systems

The challenge is **how** to reach those who remain invisible in the data. Understanding who is missing, and understanding the variations across and within countries are important first steps. Research points to the inadequacy of many health information systems to play this intended role. In some countries, information about large percentages of the population is not recorded in whole or in part due to the lack of functioning civil registration systems for births, deaths, and marriages. When data is captured mainly in facilities such as schools, clinics, and hospitals, there will inevitably be biases and gaps because those who cannot access these facilities go 'uncounted'. Dysfunctional health information systems render these groups invisible, meaning that their basic health needs are likely to go unmet.

Data fragmentation is also a major concern. Typically, a range of stakeholders, including federal and state governments, municipal actors, international donors, and a mix of local and international non-governmental organizations (NGOs), are independently involved in healthcare planning and delivery with little coordination. Regularly, health facility personnel are obliged to undertake time-consuming data collection and recording activities for different projects, but the data are then stored in separate health information systems, leading to gaps and duplication.

Confronting health inequities

The Ugandan lawsuit [see p. 1] raises questions about the role of root causes in the deaths of the two women. In explaining their court case, the Center for Health, Human Rights and Development (CEHURD) (2011: 30) noted that the majority of women cannot access services and consequently deliver "outside of health facilities and without professional attendants." They contended (p. 31) that "most deaths are preventable, and are influenced by a complex interaction of social, economic, cultural, physical environment, health seeking behaviours and quality of health delivery services." Although health fees had been abolished in the early 2000s (Dugger 2011), important questions remain about why a 40-year-old mother of seven was not sent to a more specialized centre long before the complication arose and why no one had discovered that she was carrying twins. Both women had managed to reach a health facility but they did not obtain quality care given the lack of supplies, insufficient numbers of adequately trained and motivated health workers, and, in Sylvia Nalubowa's case, demands for additional informal payments that could not be paid.

Globally, there is a clear lack of affordable access to quality healthcare services. In 2010, the WHO estimated that more than 100 million people fall into poverty each year due to catastrophic health expenditures (WHO 2010: 8). Research evidence across all regions shows that families respond to the high costs of healthcare by not even seeking needed care, by going into debt, or by foregoing critical household consumption around education and food (Brearley et al. 2012: ix). This growing health inequity by the WHO as

> the **avoidable** [emphasis added] inequalities in health between groups of people within countries and between countries. These inequities arise from inequalities within and between societies. Social and economic conditions and their effects on people's

lives determine their risk of illness and the actions taken to prevent them becoming ill or treat illness when it occurs.[16]

An IDRC-supported health systems knowledge network[17] of thought leaders examined these issues and contributed to the WHO's landmark report[18] on the social determinants of health[19] (WHO et al. 2008). The report demonstrated the impact on health of

the conditions in which people are born, grow, work, live, and age, and the wider set of forces and systems shaping the conditions of daily life. These forces and systems include economic policies and systems, development agendas, social norms, social policies, and political systems.[20]

Poverty, gender, race, and ethnicity can all contribute to exclusion and disempowerment which exacerbate poor health (Iyer et al. 2008). These factors present multiple, overlapping barriers that combine to generate a vicious cycle of poor health. To bring sustainable change, efforts are needed to address these deeper structural barriers that prevent the most vulnerable, including women, children, and adolescents, from accessing quality services.

A global agenda for transforming dysfunctional health systems

The WHO has led efforts to develop strong health systems that **can** provide accessible quality healthcare to the most vulnerable. The challenge has been where and how to make strategic investments. In most health systems, great emphasis has been placed on providing medical services in more specialized hospitals. These services, however, are often inaccessible to the majority of poor people and frequently consume large percentages of national health budgets (WHO 2008: 11). The WHO championed the urgent need to strengthen primary healthcare (PHC) at the local level where people live. PHC is particularly needed to improve maternal and child health because it is at this level that essential antenatal and postnatal care, child immunization, and treatment of endemic conditions such as malaria are provided as well as referral services to more specialized care. The WHO launched PHC during the 1978 *Alma Ata Declaration*[21] (WHO 1978) and renewed the campaign with their 2008 World Health Report *Primary Health Care: Now More Than Ever.*[22] This focus complemented efforts to put health systems[23] (WHO 2000) and equitable health systems financing (WHO 2010) on the global agenda. These shifts in thinking about health systems are dovetailing with more systemic thinking about how to reach the most vulnerable women, children, and adolescents. The necessary reforms include:

- reducing exclusion and social disparities in health (universal coverage reforms);

- organizing health services around people's needs and expectations (service delivery reforms);

- integrating health into all sectors (public policy reforms);

- pursuing collaborative models of policy dialogue (leadership reforms); and

- increasing stakeholder participation. (WHO 2008)

Addressing the impact of siloed health interventions

These trends – identifying the social determinants of health and reaffirming the importance of PHC and strong health systems – responded to the growing evidence about the varying impact of vertical, siloed efforts to improve health outcomes. Since 2000, much of the funding to support health-related MDGs in LMICs had been mobilized through a small number of Global Health Initiatives (GHIs), funded by a mix of private philanthropy and multilateral and bilateral donors. GAVI (formerly the Global Alliance for Vaccines and Immunization); the Global Fund to Fight AIDS, TB and Malaria (known simply as the Global Fund); the United States President's Emergency Plan for AIDS Relief

(PEPFAR); and the World Bank's Multi-Country AIDS Program (World Bank MAP) focused on individual diseases or health interventions and played a major role in directing investment. For example, there was a concerted effort to improve child health (MDG 4) through vaccinations with increased funding to GAVI from the Gates Foundation, and the US and UK governments. By 2015, vaccine funding amounted to 45% of the total amount of child health funding (IHME 2016: 51).

The GHIs did play an important role in helping countries meet their MDG targets – for example, by 2015, about 77% of pregnant women living with HIV had access to antiretroviral medicines to prevent transmission of HIV to their babies (UNAIDS 2016). But these measurable gains may be hard to sustain; they are often the low-hanging fruit and have not always reached the most vulnerable in society. In 2003, the Canadian International Immunization Initiative, Phase 2 – funded through IDRC – supported a series of country studies[24] that underscored the "fallacy of coverage". The studies documented ways in which the coverage and efficacy of vaccinations were undermined by a range of factors, including poorly-timed and age-inappropriate vaccinations; persistent gender gaps that meant girls were vaccinated at lower rates; and resistance by families who did not understand or accept vaccination as being consistent with their beliefs and values. The studies highlighted the dangers of assuming that reported national rates of immunization reflected actual coverage rates, with great variation seen at the local and regional levels (Mhatre and Schryer-Roy 2009).

The side effects of a singular focus on individual diseases and interventions have become apparent in the fragmentation of the overall systems. In a series of 21 country case studies published in 2009, the Maximizing Positive Synergies Academic Consortium[25] examined the impact of GHIs (mainly PEPFAR and the Global Fund) on health systems in LMICs. They found a demonstrable expansion of key services prioritized in the programs given the addition of significant new resources. On the other hand, they also found that already limited personnel and resources were sometimes directed away from overall PHC to service these specific donor priorities (Maximizing Positive Synergies Academic Consortium 2009).

Pothapregada and Atun's (2009) case study on Ghana found significant strengthening of anti-retroviral service delivery, but there were strains on health monitoring and evaluation staff from the burden of reporting results through vertical, fund-related channels. Despite the new source of funding, private out-of-pocket health expenditures continued to rise as a percentage of overall health sector expenditures. Indicators of success in non-GHI-supported initiatives in maternal and child health – including antenatal care, family planning, and deliveries by skilled attendants – failed to show comparable improvements as in the prioritized health areas.

Holding those responsible to account

The Ugandan court case highlighted on p. 1 demonstrates how civil society can help to hold government institutions account-able and to strengthen health systems. Despite many challenges, the case did go through to the Constitutional Court where it was initially dismissed based on the argument that the judiciary was not competent to hear cases related to government resource allo-cation. In October 2015, however, the Supreme Court overturned the judgment and ordered the Constitutional Court to hear the case. A new panel of judges argued that the case had raised important questions that "needed constitutional interpretation for the people of Uganda" (Mulumba 2016). While the court case continues, the government has dramatically increased funding for the health sector from US$ 215 million to US$ 328 million, recruited more health workers, and started to repair maternity wards. These investments have contributed to a reduction in maternal deaths from 420 deaths for every 100,000 live births in 2010 to 343 by 2015.[26]

This development is an important "win" but it is also necessary to identify and strengthen accountability for maternal health at sub-national levels. Through participatory action research (PAR) in three districts of Uganda, Ekirapa–Kiracho et al. (2016) found that diverse stakeholders have a role to play in improving maternal health.

> [...] local leaders (chairpersons, sub county chiefs, council members) were the entry point into the communities and they played key roles in the mobilisation of communities for community dialogues and sensitisation of the communities about the advantages of saving [money] as a means of birth preparedness. They also played key roles in holding providers such as the district health officers and facility managers accountable.

> At the household level, the involvement of men in maternal health-related issues was very crucial because they hold the economic power and are the decision makers in the family and so they influence the actions taken by their wives. (Ekirapa–Kiracho et al. 2016: 102)

In terms of the poor quality of services, much of the blame is laid at the feet of the individual health workers, but it is important to understand the drivers of uncaring behaviour and attitudes. In Ghana, Aberese-Ako et al. applied ethnographic approaches to explore frontline worker realities and found that most employees felt that various aspects of the systems they work in were unjust. Factors included poor conditions of service, perceived inequity in the distribution of incentives, and a lack of protection and respect. Unequal power relations and distrust amongst staff contributed to conflicts. The need for "creating a sense of fairness in governance arrangements between frontline workers, facilities and health system managers" was critically important (Aberese-Ako et al. 2014: ii15).

Accountability for health outcomes also extends to the global level. Back in Uganda, the increases in the national health budget still fall short of the 15% of total budget target that was committed to when the Government signed the 2001 Abuja Declaration on HIV/AIDS, Tuberculosis and Other Related Infectious Diseases[27] (WHO, Regional Office for Africa 2017). It is important to note that the health budget depends on allocations made by the Ministry of Finance, Planning and Economic Development. A report by Action for Global Health (2010)[28] found that at the time of the deaths at the heart of the CEHURD court challenge, the Government was highly dependent on external funding. Its emphasis was on macroeconomic priority-setting, which usually results in decreased public sector spending. A key finding and recommendation in the report was for donors to reflect on how their investments and criteria can negatively affect policy and spending in social sectors such as health:

> *EU [European Union] donors need to engage in a dialogue with the IMF and the World Bank, by involving governments in developing countries, in order to promote policy coherence between government, EU and non-EU donor policies – specifically with regard to sector expenditure ceilings which are believed to burden developing countries' social sectors. (Action for Global Health 2010: 5)*

These examples demonstrate that accountability is needed from the household level through to district, national, and global levels. How do we achieve this wider social responsibility for maternal and child health and health system quality more generally? Perhaps part of the solution lies in raising social awareness and supporting stakeholder advocacy about the issues at all levels.

Making the case for universal health coverage

I regard universal health coverage as the single most powerful concept that public health has to offer. It is inclusive. It unifies services and delivers them in a comprehensive and integrated way, based on primary health care. (Dr Margaret Chan, Former WHO Director-General)[29]

As we have noted earlier, the provision of accessible quality care is essential to promoting women's, children's, and adolescents' health. Global consensus that disparities in access to quality care should be eliminated were central to the World Health Assembly resolution on the need for UHC that was adopted in 2005. UHC means that

all people can use the promotive, preventive, curative, rehabilitative and palliative health services they need, of sufficient quality to be effective, while also ensuring that the use of these services does not expose the user to financial hardship.[30]

Transforming health systems to provide quality, accessible, and affordable care to the most vulnerable requires effective implementation of strategies and allocation of resources. For sustainable change, those responsible for driving such processes need to generate evidence to support healthcare financing reforms. The WHO Assembly specifically noted the need for methodologies

to measure and analyze the benefits and cost of different practices in health financing, covering collection of revenues, pooling, and provision or purchasing of services, taking account of economic and sociocultural differences.

In response, WHO's *World Health Report 2013 - Research for Universal Health Coverage*[31] set the agenda (WHO 2013). As well, an active UHC coalition[32] has brought together over 860 organizations across 117 countries, including multilateral and funding organizations, development NGOs, and civil society organizations.

This broader holistic understanding of healthcare is reflected in SDG 3: Ensure healthy lives and promote well-being for all at all ages.[33] The fragmentation caused by having separate MDGs for diseases and groups of people is overcome by integrating targets for maternal and child health and HIV under this goal. Importantly, UHC is included as a target: **Achieve universal health coverage, including financial risk protection, access to quality essential healthcare services and access to safe, effective, quality and affordable essential medicines and vaccines for all.** This changed perspective was eloquently expressed by Michel Sidibé, Executive Director of UNAIDS:

> *UHC is a cornerstone of these rights and the right to health, with protection against financial hardship at its heart. This is why UHC must be more than a technical exercise. UHC is, and must be, about realising rights and redistributing opportunity. And, as such, it is inherently political – it is about addressing entrenched power structures and tackling disempowerment, marginalisation, and exclusion. (Sidibé 2016: e355)*

Part 1 has reviewed important systemic issues that affect efforts to improve the health of the vulnerable, including women, children, and adolescents. Lack of quality disaggregated data and weak health information systems can render marginalized groups invisible, particularly if they do not visit health centres. This has dire consequences for monitoring reproductive, maternal, and child health and for planning, developing, and funding relevant programs. Structural health inequities result from a complex interaction of social, economic, and political determinants that are disproportionately borne by women and children. In response, the WHO and global stakeholders have led global efforts to transform health systems to provide accessible and affordable quality services at the primary care level and to adopt UHC strategies to sustain this change. UHC, in effect, provides the global roadmap for finding sustainable solutions to improving overall health outcomes – including maternal, child, and reproductive health and rights. Importantly, the global community has now recognized that achieving UHC is not a technical exercise but requires a political process to overcome the entrenched power divides and structural barriers that perpetuate health inequities.

Part 2

IDRC's approach to supporting health systems research

With more than a decade of supporting health systems research in LMICs, IDRC has deepened its understanding of both the needs and benefits of strong health systems. From early explorations in 2002-2006, the Centre supported three phases of funding for research and capacity development, and between 2006 and 2015 – in collaboration with like-minded donors – supported some 165 health system research projects, valued at over CA\$ 170 million.[34] The investments aimed to strengthen the ability of researchers, healthcare workers, decision-makers, and health system advocates to generate and use evidence to support stronger systems and enhance PHC. Efforts were primarily led by experts from LMICs, drawing on their intimate knowledge and experience within the specific local and regional context.

When IDRC started supporting health research in 2002, it looked beyond the global MDG targets and vertical disease or health-service specific interventions. It understood that health was both a technical and a political issue.

IDRC's health programming approach: the three effective principles

In the context of increasingly simplistic approaches to development aid that focused on immediate results, and informed by strong evidence based on supported research that examined health within a socio-political framework, IDRC sharpened its approach and applied three specific effective principles to frame its support for health systems strengthening — governance, equity, and systems integration. At the core of the approach was a recognition of the need for strong, well-governed, and equitable health systems that could serve as a foundation for the treatment and prevention of ill-health, for addressing health inequity and wider social injustice, and as an important element of sustainable development.

Governance

Governance refers to the institutions, processes, and traditions that determine how power is exercised, how decisions are made, and how citizens have their say. By shaping the way health systems are financed, designed, and implemented, governance processes play a strong role in determining the quality, quantity, and equity of health services. These processes include everything from the global structures supporting health research and investments, to the ways in which communities and households manage priorities and resources.

Equity

Equity in health involves addressing differences in health status that are unnecessary, avoidable, and unfair. Initiatives for health equity seek to allocate resources to those in greatest need. This means looking at the social determinants of health to understand the root causes of health inequity. This also includes influencing the distribution of social and economic resources to ensure health interventions promote equity.

continued...

People (users, providers, decision-makers) are at the centre of these three cross-cutting principles. Each principle both shapes and is shaped by stakeholders in the health system who share responsibilities for ensuring provision of quality accessible services. **Governance** enables citizens to set priorities and hold decision-makers and institutions accountable for their roles and responsibilities. **Equity** reveals the vulnerable people in a society and highlights the role citizens, decision-makers, and institutions have in working for a fair distribution of resources. **Health systems** include both health workers and decision-makers who provide services as well as users and advocates who demand and use the services.

Figure 2. IDRC's health programming approach – the three effective principles

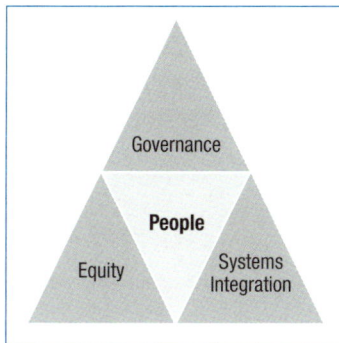

Source: Author

Effective principles link closely to Michael Quinn Patton's work on developmental evaluation, which addresses complex dynamic environments. Rather than being prescriptive, the three effective principles were intended to provide guidance that was to be interpreted, applied, and adapted to differing contexts (Patton 2011: 167).

In practice, research projects supported by IDRC addressed governance by seeking to unpack the dynamics of power and dealing with the structural issues of health and development. The projects supported the involvement and interaction of stakeholders at all levels, especially communities, in the decision-making related to the health system and their own health. They focused on equity by studying and addressing the barriers to accessing health services and how they affected those most in need – in particular, by examining gender considerations and the social determinants of health[35] which drive marginalization and exclusion. Lastly, they addressed systems integration by examining the interconnections among users and providers/decision-makers and among the various components of the health system. The projects took a more holistic approach to health by looking beyond interventions that narrowly targeted specific illnesses, services, or groups.

IDRC took a holistic approach when applying the principles. It supported LMIC research teams and institutions to develop and use relevant research methodologies to generate a scientifically rigorous body of knowledge. It also invested in a variety of strategies to enable stakeholders to use the resulting evidence to inform and influence policies, practices, agendas, and funding priorities for stronger and more equitable health systems, thereby contributing to improved health outcomes.

Developing methods and capacities to generate rigorous evidence

As noted by the WHO (2013: xv), the knowledge base to support health systems strengthening and policy change is weak. The emerging field of health policy and systems research was criticized for its unclear scope, lack of methodological rigour, and the limitations of drawing conclusions from one country context and applying them to others (Mills 2012).

To address these issues, IDRC has supported researchers working at the cutting edge of health systems research to contribute to advancing the development and application of relevant methodologies, as the examples below illustrate.

Forging new research methods

- In Niger, researchers with Laboratoire d'étude et de recherches sur les dynamiques sociales et le développement local (LASDEL)[36] have integrated qualitative collective rapid community assessment methodologies into health systems research. This is a significant contribution in Francophone West Africa, where public health research tends to be heavily quantitative.

- EQUINET, the Regional Network on Equity in Health in East and Southern Africa, has strengthened PAR methodologies and frameworks[37] as part of health systems research (Loewenson et al. 2014). The ethical foundation on which PAR has been developed explicitly recognizes the power dynamics between researchers and the communities they work with, which are often marginalized.

- The Global Network for Health Equity (GNHE)[38] has developed comprehensive methodologies for analyzing and advancing UHC.

- CIET[39] has harnessed the power of randomized controlled trials to surface and address the underlying drivers of HIV/AIDS.

Strengthening the capacity of individual researchers

IDRC has invested in building the capacities of a cadre of researchers to effectively research health systems by funding awards and fellowship programs. A host of organizations have administered these opportunities, including Institut Supérieur des Sciences de la Population,[40] The African Doctoral Dissertation Research Fellowship (ADDRF) program,[41] Collaboration for Health Systems Analysis and Innovation (CHESAI),[42] Society for Community Health Awareness Research and Action (SOCHARA),[43] and the Consortium for Mothers, Children, Adolescents, and Health Policy and Systems Strengthening (CoMCAHPSS).[44]

Generating new knowledge

Supported research has generated a significant body of new knowledge on equity, governance, and systems integration. Part 3 lays out some of the significant bodies of new evidence, including:

- causes of maternal death in rural India, where underlying issues are often masked in autopsy reports;

- hopeful new strategies to prevent HIV/AIDS in Southern Africa;

- approaches demonstrating how marginalized indigenous communities in Guatemala can hold their health systems' authorities to account; and

- system bottlenecks and implementation challenges in West Africa that are undermining health financing policies aimed at widening access to health services.

Strengthening the use of evidence to increase accountability

Even rigorous evidence will not improve people's lives unless it is used to inform the actions of those who can do something about the immediate problem. IDRC's experience has shown that following a conventional policy influence pathway – undertaking research, producing a policy brief, holding a workshop, and publishing findings in peer-reviewed journals – is too often ineffective in contributing to change. Efforts have to respond to challenges and opportunities that are specific to each context (Carden 2009). Instead, the Centre supports strategic and responsive efforts to influence policy and practice. Pioneering efforts have taken root: for example, the University of Makerere College of Health Sciences[45] has developed an innovative rapid response service to quickly provide evidence needed by senior decision-makers and parliamentarians in Uganda.

Translating new knowledge into concrete recommendations for policy and practice requires strong capacities on the part of both producers and users of evidence. Building this capacity often entails the establishment and nurturing of knowledge translation (KT) platforms that facilitate the ongoing engagement of researchers and decision-makers. In SSA, to institutionalize the uptake of research evidence, IDRC has helped establish a network of KT platforms and worked to strengthen individual country teams, including their organizational structures, their human capacity, and their use of innovative KT tools and platforms. These country teams include important stakeholders such as representatives of national ministries of health, universities, and civil society organizations along with other leading individuals.

Researchers have also understood the need to move beyond research into communication, advocacy, and political processes in order to encourage change. John-Pierre Olivier de Sardan of LASDEL noted:

> *This is where we leave behind our quest for neutrality as researchers and don our citizens' hats. In the course of its implementation, our research is as impartial and 'objective' as possible. But we select topics that involve real political and social issues at the outset and we hope that our findings will*

be used by reformers in their – mostly latent but sometimes open – battle with the conservative force. [...] It is difficult to see how the healthcare system can be improved and better quality of service provided without starting from a rigorous diagnosis of these usually concealed realities. Such diagnosis gives arguments to reformers within the health system to make change happen. (Olivier de Sardan 2015: 5)

Research organizations have found ways to engage effectively with users at the community level, with decision-makers at the local and national levels, and with influential actors at the global level. They have integrated these important stakeholders into the design and implementation of the research, they have created spaces for dialogue and debate, and, most importantly, they have built relationships of trust that make it possible to share evidence about sensitive issues and to collaborate on solutions.

This strategy has resulted in significant measures to improve the health of vulnerable women, children, and adolescents. Thanks to some of the research explored further in Part 3, the Government of India introduced new national guidelines for reviewing the causes of maternal deaths. The Government of Botswana is reorienting its entire national development programming to address the drivers of the HIV/AIDS epidemic that most affect adolescent girls and young women. The states of Bauchi and Cross River in Nigeria have worked to institutionalize evidence-based planning processes based on their experience in generating and using quality data around maternal and child health. Several governments in East and Southern Africa have used equity analyses to better address the needs of the most vulnerable, and are reporting regularly on their health equity progress to their mandated regional health body, the East, Central, and Southern African Health Community.

Part 3

Using health systems research to build healthy lives

As noted in Part 1, strong, accountable, and equitable health systems are increasingly recognized as an essential foundation for positive health outcomes for women, children, adolescents, and communities as a whole. Progress in meeting global targets for reproductive, maternal, and child health has been undermined by a myriad of long-standing health system problems in countries where the challenges are greatest.

In this section, we examine the results of IDRC's sustained support for health systems research in LMICs. We anchor the presentation of these findings around three key areas that research suggests are essential to health systems' capacity to promote equitable and effective care for vulnerable populations, including women, children, and adolescents. These areas are:

1. Data and health information systems, which play essential roles in identifying the vulnerable and in diagnosing and addressing the root causes of their poor health outcomes;

2. UHC that provides accessible quality care for all and is sustained through equitable financing that ensures financial protection for the vulnerable; and

3. Accountability, through enabling communities, institutions and health systems decision-makers to play an effective role in ensuring resources are allocated fairly and strategically.

This section shares the efforts and evidence of stakeholders working nationally, regionally, and globally to address these issues.

Strengthening data and health information systems

Reaching and improving the health of the most vulnerable women, children, and adolescents demands quality data and health information systems so that we understand who and where they are, their burden of disease, and their major health risks. It means addressing the underlying drivers that systematically fuel discrimination and exclusion.

In India, improved maternal death reviews are revealing the systematic neglect of women's health needs in pregnancy and childbirth, and the tendency of health professionals to mask their own failures; in Botswana, better data collection has enabled the government to pinpoint vulnerable youth most at risk of HIV infection and redirect resources to this group; and in Nigeria, improved household data gathering and routine use of evidence in decision-making has allowed local and state governments to determine and tackle the underlying causes of poor maternal and child health.

In India: Pinpointing the causes of maternal death

In Karnataka State, many girls and women face barriers stemming from gender-based discrimination, poverty, and caste. With a high proportion of young women malnourished and underweight for their age, and married and pregnant in their teens, risky pregnancies are more the norm than the exception. The challenge has been to develop research methods that shed light not only on the underlying medical issues affecting young pregnant women, but the complex intersections of gender, caste, and economic class that make them vulnerable to poor health and teen pregnancy. Since 2003, the Indian Institute of Management Bangalore (IIMB),[46] based in Karnataka State, has pioneered and applied ground-breaking, intersectional research methods (Iyer et al. 2008; Sen et al. 2009; Sen and Iyer 2012; Sen and Iyer 2016), including a gender analytical framework, in its community-level and health systems research in 67 village sites in the Koppal district. The results shed new light on both the medical and social determinants of maternal death.

Initial research revealed serious signs of bias and oversight in diagnosing and responding to the underlying causes of maternal death. The team reviewed the maternal death review (MDR) process – an important tool used within the health system. MDRs are intended to monitor why mothers die and to examine the degree of effectiveness or failure of health interventions. To be of use, however, the information must be accurate and comprehensive. Caution is particularly needed where those conducting the reviews may be the same healthcare providers implicated in the immediate causes of death.

IIMB discovered that, in Koppal district, official autopsies were regularly conducted by the single medical officer involved in the patient's treatment. Researchers developed an enhanced methodology in which they interviewed all key witnesses to each woman's pregnancy and emergency care. This broader approach allowed for triangulation of different narratives about the same death, thereby supporting greater accuracy in identifying causes of death (Iyer, Sen, and Srivathsa 2013). IIMB carried out verbal autopsies for 79 maternal deaths that occurred in the project area district between 2008 and 2014. They then compared their findings with those from 16 official verbal autopsies completed throughout the district after women died during, or shortly after, childbirth (between April 2008 and March 2011).

The review suggested that oversights and bias may be routinely masking the underlying causes of women's deaths. Of the 16 official reports examined, two-thirds were found to have errors in pinpointing the medical cause of death. For example, while women in Karnataka suffer high rates of nutrition-related anemia – which increases their risk during pregnancy – such common underlying conditions were not recorded. None of the official forms noted lapses by health providers, even though the review suggested they were wholly or partly responsible for three-quarters of the deaths. Health provider lapses such as the inability to recognize an emergency, the provision of inappropriate obstetric care, and negligent or inhumane treatment that caused the deaths of five women were instead attributed to the women's families (Iyer, Sen, Sreevathsa, and Varadan 2012).

IIMB's verbal autopsies highlighted the importance of earlier and more careful tracking and response by the health system to pregnant women's clinical needs. Women appeared to be dying of preventable causes because, for instance, their anemia or hypertension was not taken seriously or caught and treated early enough. These underlying causes had in effect been 'normalized' and rendered invisible to the system. The research also detailed the poor quality of care during labour and delivery, and the extent of disrespect and abuse in labour rooms. This was exacerbated when facilities were crowded, when there were staff shortages, and inadequate supervision (Iyer, Sen, and Sreevasthsa 2013). Poor post-partum practices in the community, such as restricting the women's intake of fluids or mobility, and keeping mothers and newborns in closed, smoke-filled rooms, were also shown to exacerbate the harm done by the health system's neglect of post-partum care.

New national guidelines for MDRs were introduced in India during 2010, calling for wider community input. However, IIMB's findings suggest that they may not go far enough to address inherent power imbalances confronting maternal health.

MDR interviews are still to be undertaken by the attending doctor, with latitude to reconcile competing versions of events, rather than recording conflicting versions. Without third-party oversight, the self-interest of the investigating doctor may lead to information being suppressed, and distortions in the analyses of medical and social causes of death.

IIMB acted on the research findings by working with stakeholders to develop relevant diagnostic tools to detect anemia and other health risks; develop training materials; and strengthen the capacity of frontline health workers in the pilot communities. These efforts could support health workers who had experienced a sharp increase in pressure from the mandated increase in institutional deliveries under the National Health Mission. They also took the evidence back to these same communities through a series of creative community awareness and outreach events that put shared responsibility for the health of mothers at the centre of community life. The events celebrated maternal safety and helped communities learn from maternal deaths. They included popular theatre presentations, village processions, and small group discussions, involving all who played a role in supporting healthy motherhood. A play was developed to frame the issues of child marriage and the dangers of ignoring common maternal risks such as anemia and gestational hypertension.

IIMB also created support groups within villages to accompany women during pregnancy and in the postpartum period. Members took the lead in organizing blood donations, nutrition camps, and special days focused on maternal health and safety. Additionally, they discouraged unsafe traditional practices, accompanied pregnant women to the health centre, and helped them negotiate with health staff. Some groups faced an uphill struggle where gender discrimination and superstition dominated, where power dynamics were slow to change, and where poverty contributed to a sense of powerlessness. Encouraging progress took place where groups actively sought out and followed up on women needing help.

In Botswana: Strengthening evidence to systematically tackle the drivers of HIV/AIDS

As discussed in Part 1, there is a powerful connection between HIV infection and maternal health. Reproductive health is at the core of this connection. Despite the tremendous investment in frontline HIV prevention strategies focusing on abstinence, monogamy, and use of condoms, the rates of new infections and pregnancies have remained high, particularly in Southern Africa where women and adolescent girls are at the heart of the epidemic. Research showed that in Botswana, 22.9% of young women and 8.3% of young men were HIV positive, as were 9.1% of women and 2.8% of men in Namibia, and 26.1% of women and 9.3% of men in Swaziland (Andersson and Cockcroft 2012).

By digging more deeply, CIET,[47] a southern research organization, found out why some young women were most vulnerable and why the HIV prevention strategies were not working for them (IDRC 2014). Researchers identified the "choice disabled"[48] – those who have little personal power or control over the timing and conditions of intimate contact that can expose them to unwanted pregnancy, HIV, and other sexually transmitted infections. In effect, the choice disabled lack the power to use conventional prevention and reproductive health strategies.

In 2008, CIET conducted a randomized controlled cluster trial among 7,464 youth aged 15 to 29 years in Namibia, Botswana, and Swaziland. The study found that, along with poverty and low levels of education, a range of interpersonal power dynamics was associated with a higher incidence of HIV: having less income and education than one's partner, experiencing sexual violence and intimate partner violence, a willingness to have sex without a condom despite a partner's suspected exposure to HIV/AIDS, and other risky behaviours like inconsistent use of condoms and having multiple partners (Andersson and Cockcroft 2012).

Choice disability had to be understood as a potentially significant driver of the AIDS epidemic, with prevention strategies tailored to meet the needs of the choice-disabled. The results suggested that rather than focus only on individual behaviour change prevention strategies, it could be important to support structural interventions aimed at influencing and changing the overall environment in which the choice-disabled lived.

CIET tested relevant interventions around strengthening a protective community environment, providing economic livelihood opportunities, and offering targeted life skills programs to adolescent girls and young women in Namibia, Botswana, and Swaziland. The interventions showed promising results in reducing new cases of HIV among young women at the pilot site in Botswana. Based in part on these findings, the Government of Botswana, in partnership with CIET, launched the Inter-ministerial National Structural Intervention Trial (INSTRUCT)[49] to tweak its development programs to respond to the needs of the most vulnerable group of young women aged 15 to 29. CIET applied the innovative step-wedge random control trial methodology[50] and complementary implementation research to test the strategies and interventions in one district to learn lessons before rolling out to other districts. The Government aims to ultimately cover the entire country.

INSTRUCT has galvanized action at different levels and across government sectors to re-orient programs to ensure they are working for and are accessible to this vulnerable group. In the first district to roll out the program, staff across ministries learned to communicate with youth, particularly young women. Male and female community facilitators along with teachers in all schools and government health education assistants implemented the *Beyond Victims and Villains* audio series[51] aimed at creating a more enabling and protective community environment.

Due to high community interest, many more men than expected became involved. And, in each community, young women participated in life skills workshops to build self-esteem and communication skills and to learn about how to access government programs. This has been one of the first efforts globally where a government mobilizes its own multi-sectoral resources to reorient numerous national programs in a coordinated, integrated, and sustainable manner to address at scale the structural drivers of HIV. The resulting evidence base can contribute to other efforts to scale-up this strategy.

In Nigeria: Building an evidence-based health system

Collecting and integrating quality data into functioning health information systems are essential to developing an evidence base that can help diagnose problems, inform appropriate policies and programs, and enable healthcare decision-makers to effectively allocate resources. There are, however, two common disconnects around data and information systems:

1. Gaps between information gathered at ground-level and what reaches higher level decision-makers, notably those who manage the health information system, and those involved in health planning and budgeting; and

2. Gaps in how processed information is fed back to people in the affected community in responding to their needs.

Over an eight-year period from 2006 to 2014, the Nigeria Evidence-based Health System Initiative (NEHSI)[52] built the evidence and experience to comprehensively transform data collection and health information systems at scale to more effectively address poor maternal and child outcomes.

NEHSI was forged from a partnership among the Government of Nigeria, IDRC, and the Government of Canada and the initiative was implemented as a joint effort with stakeholders in Bauchi and Cross River States. The research organization CIET[53] provided technical assistance and was embedded within relevant health authorities to strengthen structures and processes.

NEHSI used health information as an entry point to explore and address the root causes of maternal and child morbidity and mortality. Using health information was key to demonstrating the inequities in access to care and mobilizing stakeholders to address the gaps. NEHSI developed and implemented a comprehensive Multi-stakeholder Information and Planning System[54] to support effective data collection and analysis, while ensuring that the actionable evidence flowed back to decision-makers, families, and their communities.[55]

Collecting the data

The first step was to develop an overview of key issues at the state and local government area levels. To do this, NEHSI applied a social audit methodology[56] (Ledogar and Andersson 2002; CIET Trust 2006; Andersson 2011a; Andersson 2011b).[57, 58] Dr. Neil Andersson of the CIET Trust commented: "The idea [behind the social audit] is to produce hard evidence about what works, who is left out, and what will make up the shortfall." (Andersson 2011a: 2).

Data came from a carefully balanced random sample of census enumeration areas. Within the selected areas, all households were interviewed, whether or not they used government services. Complementing facility-based data with community-based data shed light on a portion of the population, amongst the most vulnerable in each state, who did not access health facilities for various reasons. These included distance to travel, waiting time, resources-involved, and quality of medical and non-medical treatment received. Research teams discussed findings with focus groups in the sample communities, documenting their views on potential solutions. Evidence was thus collected from the communities about what needed to be done to improve health outcomes and how, in their opinion, to do it.

The results provided insights into some of the less recognized causes of death and illness and particularly highlighted the impact of gendered relations. For example, surveys revealed that within households, pregnant women suffered from domestic violence and shouldered a heavy burden of work (Andersson et al. 2011b). The surveys also showed that the health of infants and children was threatened by a range of preventable conditions that could be addressed though better sanitation, diarrhea management, and use of bed nets (Odu et al. 2015). Women's levels of education, whether they lived in urban or rural areas, the information they received from health workers, the level of help from family members, and whether the household had motorized transport all appeared to play a role in determining why some women sought care and others did not (Omer et al. 2014). Findings suggested that there were inequities in access to treatment for malarial fever among children, even where community facilities existed, and they showed that mothers with more education and families with higher incomes were more likely to seek treatment for children with fever (Odu et al. 2015). Results from the final social audit helped planners in Bauchi to recognize that, while the rate of polio vaccination coverage was successful, it was at the expense of declines in routine immunization (Cockcroft et al. 2014).

Secondly, implementation research methods were then applied to collect additional information directly from households. Outreach workers, typically community health workers, visited and formally registered all households in the local government area and all women of child-bearing age (those between the ages of 15 and 49). The households, pregnancies, and newborns were followed. Structured survey tools were used to prompt discussions with each pregnant woman about the risks identified from the statewide social audit: domestic violence, hard work during pregnancy, and knowledge of danger signs. While female fieldworkers engaged household members in discussions focused around the care of pregnant women, male workers carried out similar discussions with husbands. Using cellular-enabled touchscreen android tablets, fieldworkers collected and relayed the geo-indexed data to a server in the State Ministry of Health headquarters. This created a real-time, live information system.

Using the data

Once the data was collected, it had to be fed back to those with the responsibility to do something about the issues raised. A third methodology, Socialising Evidence for Participatory Action,[59] fed the evidence into both community and state-level governmental structures.

Information was taken back to communities in different ways. Families with pregnant women and newborns received information directly and discussed actions to reduce risks during follow-up home visits by community health workers who continually updated the community surveillance system. Docudramas,[60] a series of dramatized short videos, brought health issues to life and informed community-based action planning. The videos were used as a basis for discussion on what measures could be taken against the domestic violence and excessive workloads experienced by many pregnant women.

As a result of the interventions, community members engaged more in health services and health planning. Community action groups, created in each focus community, carried out awareness-raising and responsive activities. Some groups, for example, mobilized and bought grinders to reduce the workload for pregnant women. Others organized transportation to hospitals and clinics, and even mobilized support to build a road, thus reducing transit time to the clinic. In this way, as happened in Koppal, India, community action groups contributed to cultural shifts in attitudes towards pregnant women and the use of the health system, and promoted proper management of childhood illnesses.

A story of change from Bauchi state

NEHSI's community-level impacts were captured in a series of *Most Significant Change* stories.[61] Here, one Bauchi husband recounts how he treated his wife, and what he learned from evidence brought back to his community through a NEHSI docudrama:

"I have lived in my community for the past 50 years. I am the Santali of Sarki (cattle holder) and I am also a tailor. I have two wives and eleven children. I am also a member of the community development group. A year before your people came I criticized, shouted, and made unnecessary complaints to my senior wife. At that point in time she was pregnant. I kept complaining even about those things that were not important. For example, I would ask her why she did that instead of this. She would mostly keep quiet. At times, she explained she was feeling weak. Gradually, she became depressed. However, I turned my eyes away from her and did not give it much thought.

When she was nine months pregnant, she was ready to deliver. When the time came, she had to endure a prolonged labour. She was rushed to the hospital where she started bleeding profusely. Finally, she gave birth to a child, but the child was not alive. The health workers put her on drips and she spent two days in the hospital. They charged me for her medical bills. All this time, I kept wondering and worrying about the cause. Why did she have to suffer like this? Finally, I prayed to Allah for an intervention.

One Sunday morning, I watched your drama at our sarki's palace. In the drama, I saw Fatima's husband and the way he behaved towards his wife. After the screening, I said to myself, 'this is what I used to do to my wife. My behavior is the reason why she lost her child.' I reached home late that day. My wives had also, by then, watched the drama. I discussed it with both of them. Then I said to my senior wife, 'please forgive me for what has happened to you.' She accepted my apology immediately. Henceforth, my life took a new turn and I began to reassess my attitudes towards her. Now I show her love and care. Some months after she got pregnant and this time around she delivered safely."

Bauchi Individual, January 2013

The social audits provided new and detailed data on the situation in each selected local government area (LGA). In turn, the data was analyzed and presented for planners in various formats, including scorecards and issue-specific fact sheets with maps using the GPS data. Scorecards[62] summarized key community health indicators such as the percentage of pregnant women visiting government health facilities, and experiencing complications. This tool enabled planners to compare health indicators across LGAs and to identify areas for improvement. Discussions on scorecard results were timed to feed into budgeting and planning cycles, so that emerging health priorities could be considered.

The initiative worked closely with decision-makers from different health institutions at local, ward, and state government levels. This strategy was integral to the institutionalization of evidence-based planning and decision-making, and NEHSI was featured in the Nigeria *Millennium Development Goals 2013 Report* (Government of Nigeria 2013: 40). In fact, Professor C.O. Chukwu, a former Honorable Minister of Health of Nigeria noted: "NEHSI is a paradigm shift on two levels: 1. focusing on evidence-based planning, and 2. results from and with communities. It is not just about data for its own sake, but rather data that informs **us**." (Government of Nigeria 2014: 28)

Decision-makers were so convinced of the value of NEHSI that a process document[63] was developed at the suggestion of the Nigerian government to help scale up the initiative to other states (Government of Nigeria 2014). It presented the fundamentals of the NEHSI approach but rather than prescribing step-by-step instructions on replicability, it shared the principles that could be implemented in different contexts.

Building the momentum for affordable universal health coverage

Financing is the most critical of all determinants in a health system. The nature of financing defines the structure, the behaviour of different stakeholders and the quality of outcomes. (Government of India 2005a: 68)

While health information systems and use of data are critical to improving maternal health, other significant barriers need to be addressed.

The decision by families to seek care, and the ability of states to provide adequate care, is influenced by many factors, but perhaps none has been more debated or studied than that of cost. For millions around the world, affordable healthcare remains a dream.

Over the years, governments of LMICs have adopted various approaches to levy funds for healthcare, often under pressure from lenders and donors. The practice of imposing user fees and insisting on direct payment for services at the time of accessing services spread quickly throughout the 1980s, in response to external funding conditionalities linked to structural adjustment policies imposed by international institutions (UNICEF 1987). For example, in 1987, most African countries signed the Bamako Initiative[64] (sponsored by UNICEF and the WHO) and adopted direct payment for healthcare services as the principal means of financing their health systems.

Research increasingly demonstrated the negative effects of fees on the use of health services, particularly by disadvantaged groups. LMICs also recognized the hardships these fees placed on vulnerable people. Facing growing pressure to attain the MDGs, and in response to new global funding priorities, many countries subsidized or abolished direct payment for specific health services (such as HIV treatment) and for specific groups (such as pregnant women and children under the age of five).

As illustrated below, researchers are documenting the reform efforts around healthcare fees. In West Africa, selected subsidies on maternal and child health have had unintended consequences in reducing quality of care. The Indian state of Andhra Pradesh's innovative insurance scheme to increase its citizens' access to specialized medical services underscored the need for broader coverage for vulnerable families at the PHC level. Networks of health financing experts working in Asia, Africa, and Latin America – and collectively at the global level – have demonstrated the need for more relevant analytical health financing tools. Their evidence demonstrated the long-term impoverishing impact of out-of-pocket health expenditures on families and validated the critical need for comprehensive and integrated UHC mechanisms that provide equitable access to quality needed services along with financial risk protection.

In West Africa: Exposing unintended consequences of abolishing user fees

From 2009 to 2012, researchers led by Niger's LASDEL[65] analyzed government efforts in Burkina Faso, Mali, and Niger to increase access to maternal and child healthcare by removing user fees.[66] The data below show that despite significant gains in reducing maternal mortality, insufficient progress was being made in achieving the maternal mortality MDG.

To address maternal and child health priorities, fees were removed or reduced for treatment and prevention of HIV and malaria, caesarean sections and other deliveries, and care of pregnant women and children under five. In Niger, contraception and cancer treatment for women were also covered.

While research confirmed that removing financial barriers clearly increased the use of health services among the poorest women, poor planning and implementation threatened the quality of services provided. The ways in which fee exemptions were introduced created new demands on already weak health systems.

Table 3. Trends in estimates of maternal mortality ratio (MMR) in Burkina Faso, Mali and Niger, 1990-2015

Country	1990 MMR	2000 MMR	2015 MMR	% change in between 1990 and 2015[67]	Progress Towards MDG 5A[68]
Burkina Faso	727	547	371	49%	Insuffient progress
Mali	1010	834	587	41.9%	Insufficient progress
Niger	873	794	553	36.7%	Insufficient progress

Source: WHO et al. (2015). *Trends in maternal mortality: 1990 to 2015*. Estimates by WHO, UNICEF, UNFPA, World Bank Group and the United Nations Population Division, Annex 19, p. 70.

Researchers identified several "unintended effects" of poorly implemented policies. User fees persisted for costs not covered by "free" healthcare service along with indirect costs for transportation and food, and "under-the-counter" payments to healthcare staff. Generally, facilities had to first provide services and subsequently seek reimbursement from central Ministries of Health. Delays in reimbursement resulted in a lack of funds to buy medical supplies and medicines, which in turn forced patients to buy these privately. In particular, specially formulated syrups for children disappeared because they were too expensive. This made it difficult for mothers to correctly administer medication to their children (Diarra and Ousseini 2015: 6).

Specific public policymaking challenges were encountered by the countries trying to implement these subsidies. Often the policy decisions were announced suddenly, reflecting both international pressure and internal political concerns. There was lack of coordination among technical and financial partners who often did not know local conditions and who remained unaccountable for the consequences of their interventions. Insufficient planning and preparation of the necessary systems (e.g., speedy reimbursement mechanisms for health facility services) led to numerous bottlenecks, as vividly documented in a film[69] about the experience in Niger. A failure to monitor, to evaluate, or to take account of research data made it difficult to anticipate or address operational problems. A lack of preparation and effective communication with key actors – including health staff, health committees, local authorities, and users – led to demotivation and resistance in implementing the policies. Users, meanwhile, were unable to demand quality services. More fundamentally, there was a tendency to recentralize decisions and funding in places where the decentralization process had only just begun (Olivier de Sardan and Ridde 2015: 4). These reflections served to underline the complexity involved in bringing about sustainable change around well-intentioned policies. The evidence also pointed to the need for more comprehensive rather than piecemeal approaches to improving access to quality maternal health services.

In India: Advancing universal health coverage

As discussed in Part 1, a global consensus has created momentum toward UHC as an essential means of overcoming the poor health results associated with fragmented services, insurance gaps, out-of-pocket expenses, and user fees for services. Despite its size and complexity, India is demonstrating how progress towards UHC **can** be achieved. These comprehensive efforts are required to improve health outcomes for the vulnerable and to provide needed services, especially for reproductive, maternal, and child health.

India is the second most populous country in the world and its 1.3 billion citizens currently pay for many of their medical needs directly out of their own pockets.

Table 4. Out-of-pocket health expenditures in India

Indicator	1995	2014
Out-of-pocket health expenditure (% of total health expenditure)	67	62
Out-of-pocket health expenditure (% of private expenditure on health)	91	89

Source: WHO Global Health Expenditure Database – India
http://apps.who.int/nha/database/Select/Indicators/en

The challenges in reforming the system are daunting, and, in 2005, the National Commission on Macroeconomics and Health stated that

> the principal challenge for India is the building of a sustainable health system. Selective, fragmented strategies and lack of resources have made the health system unaccountable, disconnected to public health goals, inadequately equipped to address people's growing expectations and unable to provide financial risk protection to the poor. (Government of India 2005: 4)

Despite the challenges, considerable efforts have been made to better meet the health needs of the poorest. Research has helped to create important knowledge bases, and, in 2011, a High Level Expert Group on UHC reviewed national experiences and provided recommendations for progressively implementing UHC[70] across the country (Planning Commission of India 2011). The following examples share the insights and experience gained in methodically implementing and learning from efforts to tackle the difficult task of financing health services.

Lessons from Andhra Pradesh

In India, substantive work on health systems has to be undertaken at the state level, given their responsibility for providing healthcare. Several are testing innovative health financing solutions to improve access to care. In 2007, the state of Andhra

Pradesh introduced the Rajiv Aarogyasri Community Health Insurance Scheme (Aarogyasri) to provide universal coverage by improving access to quality specialized medical care to the urban and the rural poor in the state (Rao et al. 2014).

Aarogyasri was among the most comprehensive healthcare schemes in India. It was a state-wide and fully state-funded health insurance scheme that automatically enrolled all families falling below a specified poverty line. As a public-private partnership, 342 public and private sector hospitals were formally registered to provide services to Aarogyasri beneficiaries (Fan, Karan, and Mahal 2012).

A rapid assessment in 2008 identified gaps, however, and state officials commissioned an evaluation to identify lessons for strengthening implementation and impact. Led by the Administrative Staff College of India, starting in 2011, the evaluation confirmed many benefits of the scheme – 80% of the state population was covered and 85% of these families were aware that they were covered (Bergkvist et al. 2014). An adjusted comparison with the neighbouring state of Maharashtra suggested that the scheme increased access in Andhra Pradesh, particularly for hospital and surgery admissions per capita, and reduced the growth of out-of-pocket expenditures per admission, although this reduced growth was evident only amongst the better off (Bergkvist et al. 2014: 41-42).

At the same time, only 25% of respondents knew that the Aarogyasri benefit package covered a specific list of high-cost procedures and up to 60% thought that all health issues were covered. Many did not know about or claim available entitlements such as a transport subsidy or follow-up care after discharge. About 14% of those surveyed had been denied financial support by Aarogyasri, most often because their condition was not covered (Bergkvist et al. 2014: 42).

This had dire consequences for the poorest. In-depth case studies documented how some patients continued to incur large out-of-pocket expenses – and went into debt – for interventions that they had believed would be covered under the Aarogyasri insurance program. The case studies pointed to a widespread lack of confidence among vulnerable populations to seek information about how to use the system and to the "mistrust and fear about state healthcare facilities and schemes" in general (Narasimhan 2014: 94). An important reflection was that the scheme focused only on specialized medical care, displacing primary prevention. In addition, hospitalization was required to cover the cost of medication. For the poorest, all healthcare needs could easily result in financial and social ruin, especially in the most vulnerable households. The authors concluded that "[f]or a public health finance scheme to be effective in a country such as India, it has to widen its definition" to include services such as maternal and child health services (Narasimhan 2014: 95). They urged leaders to examine the persistent financial and non-financial barriers and to use evidence to design a UHC strategy that was accessible to all (Narasimhan 2014: 96). They also reflected on the need for free quality PHC (Narasimhan 2014: 94).

This experience shows how the specific health needs of disadvantaged groups can be 'forgotten' and why the issues around reproductive, maternal, and child health need to be centrally embedded in planning processes.

Strengthening state capacity to implement Universal Health Coverage
Building on this body of evidence, the Public Health Foundation of India (PHFI) has worked since 2013 with several state-level institutions and decision-makers to prepare for a phased roll out of UHC through defining and projecting costs for a much broader state-flexible Essential Health Package.[71] A resulting draft framework[72] covers 492 healthcare services – from health promotion to palliative care – under four broad categories, including

women's and children's health; communicable and non-communicable diseases; and selected broader determinants of health (Bhatt et al. n.d.). PHFI has also supported states in estimating treatment costs and defining integrated care pathways for the management of diseases that account for the greatest costs and burden of disease. The practical, evidence-based guidance developed by the PHFI aims to help Indian states expand UHC in a sustainable way that may serve as a model for other LMICs.

At the global level: Regional networks advance Universal Health Coverage

As noted by the WHO in 2013, one of the priority needs for advancing toward UHC is the generation of relevant research and evidence. Identifying methodologies to analyze financial mechanisms to fund universal coverage remains a particular challenge. UHC puts vulnerable people at the centre of the equation but most methodologies are not sensitive to specific groups, such as those requiring reproductive, maternal, and child healthcare services. Between 2006 and 2011, three regional health financing networks in Latin America, Asia, and Africa focused on methodologies to strengthen equity and create the fiscal space for covering the costs of a relevant package of health services. Individually and collectively, the networks built a substantive evidence base to inform countries, and contributed significantly to the global discourse on advancing UHC.

Between 2008 and 2011, Equity in Asia-Pacific Health Systems (EQUITAP)[73] consolidated knowledge in 20 countries about the scale and impact on families of out-of-pocket expenditures. Through its studies, EQUITAP assessed the value of data generated through existing tools such as national household expenditure surveys and identified a number of methodological and conceptual challenges. This was an important contribution to the discourse on methodologies and the support needed by national governments to effectively implement universal coverage.

The study (Rannan-Eliya et al. 2012) demonstrated that the national household expenditure surveys were a significant source of evidence and data on the barriers facing households in accessing healthcare and the financial impacts of out-of-pocket expenditures. This meant the data could be used to assess these problems without having to commission expensive new surveys. There were, however, significant limits to the evidence generated through these surveys. In particular, methodological inconsistencies made it difficult to undertake comparative studies over time and across countries. Costs needed to be clearly and commonly defined and consistently measured. There was potential for progress in this area given that more LMICS were compiling internationally comparable measures of health spending using a national health accounts framework (Rannan-Eliya et al. 2012: 25).

More fundamentally, it was recognized that most surveys would not generate sufficient sample sizes to separately analyze maternal out-of-pocket expenditures because utilization of maternal healthcare happens relatively infrequently during a woman's life. Either much larger samples or separate specialized surveys would be needed. And, as in earlier examples, existing data left out many births because they took place at home and were not counted (Rannan-Eliya et al. 2012: 25).

A great limitation was that existing research focused largely on antenatal and pregnancy care costs without considering the indirect costs of accessing care (Brearley et al. 2012). For example, families incurred significant opportunity costs in taking time to obtain needed care as well as in disruption in income-generation through caring for sick family members. The research confirmed that, in most countries, these combined financial and time costs of accessing maternal and child healthcare often contributed to household impoverishment. Universal coping strategies were used, such as borrowing money and reducing consumption of food or education, resulting in a long-term negative impact that extended far beyond the initial direct costs. Because the time frame used in most maternal, newborn, and child health (MNCH) care cost surveys was too short, investment in longitudinal surveys of households was essential to examine these longer-term effects of catastrophic MNCH healthcare payments (Brearley et al. 2012: 32).

EQUITAP found that only some surveys incorporated detailed health modules querying illness, reasons for not seeking healthcare when sick, and types and costs of healthcare provision utilized. They concluded that even if the existing health modules were improved, they would not be able to provide comprehensive data on all barriers to healthcare. A final recommendation was therefore that work on MNCH care costs should draw from the poverty literature and its multidimensional measures of household welfare. Combining more systematic health spending surveys with better-designed national consumption surveys could help to more realistically define MNCH cost levels and financial impact (Brearley et al. 2012: 32).

Similar research was undertaken in Latin America which has long dealt with inequitable access to healthcare services and limited financial protection for the poor. In 2012, the Latin American Research Network on Equity and Health Systems (LAnet-EHS) published *Financing Health in Latin America*[74] (Knaul et al. 2012) to share their substantial findings on the levels and determinants of catastrophic health expenditures across the region. The key research question was whether supported reforms and developed mechanisms had effectively provided financial protection against health and financial risk.

This research significantly strengthened the evidence base on health spending and impoverishment across the region. For the first time, it consolidated data for nine countries and undertook a comparative study across Argentina, Brazil, Chile, Colombia, Costa Rica, Dominican Republic, Guatemala, Mexico, and Peru, which together account for 85% of Latin America's population. The findings confirmed that, due to high levels of health spending, large numbers of people, particularly the most vulnerable populations, had been pushed into poverty and had to cope with illness, economic ruin, and impoverishment. Importantly, the research identified the specific groups most vulnerable to catastrophic and impoverishing health expenditures in each country. Overall, poor rural households with children or elderly members were more vulnerable (Knaul et al. 2012: 67).

LAnet-EHS made a significant contribution to methodological innovation for the region by laying the foundation for systematic comparisons across countries. Researchers discussed limitations of existing methodologies and developed common variable definitions for units of analysis, metrics, and strategies for measurement. The Network also developed a comparative methodology. As did EQUITAP, where the researchers underlined the critical need for quality data to support longitudinal analyses of household health spending:

> [...] in addition to knowing **if, how many and which** households are experiencing catastrophic or impoverishing expenditures in health, it is critical to know **how long** households stay in a financially vulnerable position after health shocks occur, how well they recover from these shocks, and whether they eventually sacrifice health by not spending. (Knaul et al. 2012: 13)

Strategies for Health Insurance for Equity in Less Developed Countries (SHIELD Network), active in SSA, strengthened existing methodologies to advise governments on how to assess specific financing strategies. Most countries in the region have relied on some form of health insurance to finance health services. The question has been how to include those in the informal sector and the poorest who cannot afford premiums.

SHIELD applied an equity lens to explore whether it was more equitable and efficient to cover premiums "through contributory insurance schemes (with subsidies for the poorest) or through tax funding" (McIntyre and Mills 2012: i1).

Researchers evaluated the health systems in Ghana, South Africa, and Tanzania by examining the various financing mechanisms, including

> a dedicated health tax in Ghana (the National Health Insurance levy, which is an additional 2.5% on the value added tax); private voluntary health insurance contributions in South Africa; and mandatory health insurance contributions for formal sector workers and district-based health insurance contributions by those outside the formal sector in Ghana and Tanzania. (McIntyre and Mills 2012: i2)

Findings were published in a 2012 special supplement of *Health Policy and Planning*.[75] Two important overall results contributed to the global discourse on UHC.

1. **There was a critical need for UHC to encompass not only financing mechanisms but also the best ways to promote access to needed healthcare on a universal basis.** Researchers refined specific methodologies to integrate equity analyses by applying benefit incidence analysis to both private and public health services. They also challenged the prevailing assumption that the need for healthcare was the same across different socio-economic groups by applying an equity definition for service use, that of "utilization being in line with need" (McIntyre and Mills 2012: i2). Results compared the distribution of service benefits with the distribution of a measure of need for healthcare across different groups of people. The combined financing and benefit incidence analyses generated knowledge about the extent of income and risk cross-subsidies within the three countries' health systems.

2. There was a critical need to actively engage with a wide array of stakeholders to build consensus around cross-subsidizing the poor. Recognizing that universal health systems "are built on social solidarity" (Goudge et al. 2012), researchers explored the extent of public willingness to contribute to mechanisms that would cross-subsidize services for the poorest. Methodologies to analyze stakeholder views were applied in South Africa and Tanzania and the findings underlined the need to actively build consensus amongst stakeholders about UHC. The significance of this research is that it took the discourse and practice of UHC out of a narrow, mainly economic technical discussion to a broader political and social process requiring the input of all stakeholders.

The three networks reached similar conclusions: existing tools were limited and there was an urgent need to develop more appropriate tools, including consistent definitions and indicators that could facilitate comparative studies over time and across geographical boundaries. It was necessary to move beyond analyses of direct costs to examine indirect costs and to look at access to services. There was a critical need to build stronger evidence bases, particularly with longitudinal studies to show long-term impact of health expenditures on household welfare. And finally, their efforts showed that equitable financing for UHC was not just a technical exercise but required political will and a sense of social solidarity across the population for effective implementation.

By 2011, SHIELD, EQUITAP, and LAnet-EHS had decided to join forces and collaborate as the GNHE[76] to increase their visibility and impact in the global drive for UHC.[77] GNHE argued that UHC needed to encompass both access to necessary health services of sufficient quality to be effective, and financial risk protection for all. In December 2012, the Network called upon international bodies, including the WHO and UNICEF, to recognize the need for including progress towards UHC[78] as a global development objective in the proposed SDGs.[79]

Not only have their efforts contributed to including UHC as a target under Goal 3 (Good Health and Well-being)[80] but their work is reflected in the indicators adopted by the UN Statistical Commission[81] in March 2017 to measure the target.[82]

SDG indicators to measure universal health coverage

3.8.1   Coverage of essential health services

3.8.2   Proportion of population with large household expenditures on heath as a share of total household expenditure or income

---

GNHE has also developed an integrated methodology that holistically examines health[83] based on work by McIntyre and Kutzin (2016). They proposed assessing the adequacy and equity of overall service utilization, rather than focusing on a few services (such as antenatal care and immunizations). To provide practical support to help inform the progressive realization of universal coverage for countries, GNHE has applied its methodology to a growing list of country UHC assessments.[84]

This research supports efforts to sustainably build and finance comprehensive and integrated national health systems rather than selected and fragmented services, including those for reproductive, maternal, and child health. Strong integrated national health systems can not only help to achieve improved health outcomes at scale for vulnerable populations, including women, children, and adolescents but can also help to prevent and manage major disruptions caused by disease outbreaks and other emergencies.

Integrating universal health coverage into the SDGs

The research described above contributed to a powerful evidence base that was used to keep UHC on the global agenda. The UN Secretary-General established the Sustainable Development Solutions Network[85] to provide technical support to the intergovernmental processes involved in developing the SDGs. Significantly, the thematic working group on health was co-chaired by prominent researchers funded by IDRC, including Irene Agyepong (Specialist public health researcher, Ghana Health Services) and Srinath Reddy (President, Public Health Foundation of India).[86] The Working Group deliberations reflected the growing consensus on the need for a comprehensive understanding of UHC. Their final report to the UN Secretary General[87] in 2014 stressed (p. 6) that:

> We believe that universal health coverage (UHC), delivered through an adequately-resourced and well-governed health system, will be capable of addressing these and other health challenges, especially if supported by policies in other sectors which promote health and environmental sustainability and reduce poverty. [...] Governments must play the role of both guarantor and enabler, mobilizing all relevant societal resources for the delivery of health services. National commitment to universal health coverage must be legally embedded in a rights-based framework.

> Since the determinants of health extend across multiple sectors, the post-2015 development agenda must promote synergies and partnerships that align actions for better health. Improved health of individuals and populations will also help in achieving other development goals such as poverty reduction, gender empowerment, and universal education [...]

> Apart from the intrinsic value of health, UHC can create positive externalities for development, women's empowerment and gender equity, and social solidarity. Within the health sector, primary health care should be accorded the highest importance because of its ability to provide maximum health benefits to all parts of society and to ensure sustainable health care expenditure levels. (Thematic Group on Health for All of the Sustainable Development Solutions Network 2014: 6-7)

There was also an acknowledgement that the realization of UHC would be challenging. Countries are faced with difficult choices on how to strategically allocate often-scarce resources across many competing priorities. In such situations, the needs of vulnerable women, children, and adolescents can fall through the cracks. In 2010, the World Health Assembly called on the WHO to develop an action plan to support countries seeking to enhance universal coverage. The WHO in turn asked a group of health ethicists from India, Zambia, Thailand, Uganda, Ethiopia, Norway, the UK, and the United States to develop guidelines to help countries address ethical issues while expanding universal coverage.[88] The core recommendations of the final WHO report, *Making fair choices on the path to universal health coverage*[89] (WHO 2014), lay out three kinds of strategies for countries to achieve the fair and progressive realization of UHC:

- Categorizing services into priority classes, using relevant criteria including cost-effectiveness, giving priority to the worse off, and financial risk protection;

- Expanding coverage for high-priority services to everyone to eliminate out-of-pocket payments while increasing mandatory, progressive prepayment with pooling of funds; and

- Ensuring that disadvantaged groups – typically low-income groups and rural populations – are not left behind.

Ensuring that women, children, and adolescents are not left behind

The concern about not leaving disadvantaged groups behind brings us back to the issue of women, children, and adolescents. How can the promise of UHC ensure that their needs will be met? As we saw with the Aarogyasri insurance scheme in India, important maternal and child health services were not covered.

In the special supplement around reproductive health and rights[90] referred to in the preface, Sen and Govender (2015: 235) analyzed the potential for UHC to improve SRHR and for SRHR to strengthen health systems. They cautioned against focusing narrowly on the wealth aspect of universality and argued for a focus on women and adolescents with "attention to intersecting inequalities of location, race/ethnicity/caste, disability, other status."

UHC provides a strategic window of opportunity to advance the health of women, children, and adolescents. To achieve this, Sen and Govender also cautioned against dealing with adolescents' and women's needs in silos but to rather include them centrally in planned changes with appropriate financing mechanisms to ensure their needs are met. Overall system improvements and services benefitting everyone need to be accompanied by "special attention to those whose needs are great and who are likely to fall behind" (Sen and Govender 2015: 235). Quality comprehensive sexuality education and access to SRH services need to be provided over the life course of girls and women and deal with the full range of needs. Given the frequent exclusion of married and unmarried adolescent girls from health and educational services, UHC processes need to engage in multi-sectoral action to address the underlying drivers of early and forced marriage, lack of access to schooling, and violence. Importantly, relevant benchmarking and monitoring to track progress is needed (Sen and Govender 2015: 236).

Importantly, the authors recognized that SRHR and UHC are

> shaped in turn by what may be called the politics of choice and voice – who is at the policy table, and what interests are effectively represented … UHC's major choices are almost always political and not only technical … making essential the involvement and engagement of a multiplicity of stakeholders, including not only planners and technocrats but also civil society and political leaders. (Sen and Govender 2015: 233-234)

Given these challenges, how can governments and stakeholders build the consensus for developing sustainable health systems that will ensure equitable and affordable access to quality services for all, without leaving anyone behind?

Researchers and stakeholders have shared lessons and reflections captured in the next section.

Building sustainable and equitable health systems through strengthening accountability and governance

The evidence has demonstrated how the needed services for vulnerable groups can be fragmented and of poor quality. There is a critical need to strengthen accountability, governance, and stewardship of health resources to help ensure that decisions and resource allocations are strategically and consistently made to sustainably address the health needs of vulnerable populations. This requires that the broad array of health system actors assume their particular responsibilities – from the community to global levels. Unless quality services are accessible and affordable to people at the point of service delivery, a health system is not working properly. Users need to engage in monitoring the systems and in holding to account those who have a responsibility for delivering the services.

The next examples illustrate how researchers and stakeholders in Guatemala, South Africa, and Uganda have worked with vulnerable communities to hold authorities accountable for services provided. Efforts paid off and, for example, led to improved maternal child health services in participating communities in rural Uganda. In East, Central, and Southern Africa, EQUINET's experience shows how it is possible to strengthen governance at scale through working with authorities to monitor the level of equity in national health systems and to enable collective regional monitoring. Their research also put evidence on the table about systemic global factors that have a negative impact on efforts to improve health services, including those for women, children, and adolescents. And finally, we look at how researchers, practitioners, and decision-makers are building the relationships of trust needed to enable the exchange of critical views that is essential to strengthening governance and creating accountable and responsive health systems.

In Guatemala: Building indigenous oversight of health system performance

Despite its middle-income status, Guatemala has one of the highest MMRs in Latin America – 88 deaths for every 100,000 live births – compared with an overall average MMR of 67 for the continent (WHO et al. 2015). Among those with the worst health outcomes are the country's rural indigenous people. This group was traumatized by decades of civil war that included widespread torture and assassinations perpetrated by government forces. The violence left the population with deep psychological and social scars, created a pervasive distrust of authorities and institutions, and undermined social and political participation. Among the targets of government repression were local and community leaders, including health promoters and traditional midwives, rural teachers, and agricultural extension workers – in short, the very people who would typically catalyze civic action and development in rural communities (Flores, Ruano, and Funchal 2009). These losses have been a major factor in keeping indigenous communities from asserting their rights, including the right to quality health services.

While progressive legal reforms enacted since the end of the war have aimed to end discrimination, rural communities – and indigenous populations in particular – have continued to receive inferior treatment and services through the country's patchwork of health clinics. Among the most common complaints have been the lack of respect received from health workers and authorities, frequent shortages of medication and other supplies, and unreliable clinic hours.

By informing and educating indigenous communities on their health rights, and engaging members as citizens at the heart of health monitoring systems, Centro de Estudios para la Equidad y Gobernanza en los Sistemas de Salud[91] has been equipping people to assert their rights, demand accountability, and regain essential skills for civic participation.[92] First field-tested in six rural municipalities between 2006 and 2010, the monitoring system has now been extended to 20 additional rural municipalities. In phase 1, local committees collected and analyzed information on health service performance four times a year and then reported results to their municipal development commission. From their discussions, action plans were developed. The steering committee then monitored whether activities identified within the action plans were carried out. Findings fed into successive cycles of assessment and fine tuning to ensure that this joint action was improving equitable access and accountability.[93]

In phase 2, efforts began with mass mobilization and training in targeted communities to raise levels of literacy on the right to health under Guatemala's legal framework. As a basis for partici-patory monitoring of health services, community members were trained in using audiovisual tools – cameras and other recording equipment – to capture evidence of right-to-health violations, and in advocacy strategies to mobilize community demands for accountability from health authorities. Researchers experimented with the use of mobile phones and crowd-sourcing data and an open source platform was launched in 2014. This enabled health service users to document and pinpoint the location of health service gaps and violations, such as a lack of supplies, staffing shortages, or ill-treatment of patients. The visual mapping on the website has been widely accessible, and provided another means of promoting accountability.

Importantly, overall power dynamics have changed. The multi-stakeholder steering committees, which include health workers and representatives from municipal government and community organizations, have helped to address the lack of trust between citizens and health authorities by bringing them together to evaluate and report on healthcare facilities and families' experiences with them. The committees have gained the confidence to engage at the national level with parliamentarians, the Ministry of Health, the National Ombudsman's Office, and other national human rights bodies. Through these processes, communities have gained greater accountability from local and national authorities. Moreover, they have seen tangible changes in the quality of care: abusive healthcare workers have been sanctioned, patients are being treated with more respect, and municipal governments have allocated funding to pay for emergency transportation and to purchase additional medication. These critical changes are needed to improve efforts to reduce the high maternal mortality rates in the communities.

In South Africa and Uganda: Strengthening citizen input on health systems

In South Africa and Uganda, the right to health is constitutionally recognized and governments have promoted community participation through the establishment of health committees. Meaningful participation in healthcare decision-making, however, has been elusive.

From 2012 to 2015, Uganda's CEHURD[94] and the University of Cape Town's School of Public Health and Family Medicine (UCT)[95] worked with health committees, civil society, and local authorities to identify ways to better equip health committees to fulfil their role in facilitating citizen input to shape responsive healthcare systems. Formative research in two rural districts in Uganda and the Cape Town Metropolitan area in South Africa documented challenges, including lack of understanding about roles and responsibilities, insufficient skills, poor communication channels, and weak linkages with other actors in the health system (London and Mulumba 2013). CEHURD and UCT provided contextualized and innovative training and capacity building programs to selected health committees, and supported networking with other civil society organizations at the local, district, national, and regional levels.

The effort produced some notable results, including for the health of mothers and children. For example, the Nyamiringa health committee in Uganda successfully petitioned district officials to make the maternity ward functional and build staff quarters. Ultimately, an additional midwife, clinician, and laboratory technician were added to the local health centre staff. Engaging with civil society at national levels made it possible to seek the intervention of the Uganda Human Rights Commission and Minister of Water to address the issues of water disconnection and a lack of water supply at a number of clinics and district hospitals. Cape Town health committees successfully engaged with officials around institutionalizing their role in Department of Health planning processes.

The findings demonstrated, however, that efforts to strengthen the capacity of health committees needed to be embedded in broader health systems strengthening strategies rather than be handled as isolated interventions. Health committees needed to be collectively linked to higher level district and metropolitan structures so that input and feedback from local levels could reach those responsible for decisions and resource allocations at regional and national levels.

In Cape Town, a learning network[96] was established for skilled and motivated members from the many individual committees. The network created opportunities for information sharing and additional capacity strengthening. As a result, it has increasingly provided a collective leadership and voice for scattered individual health committees. It has been called on by official health structures to facilitate dialogues and engagement at a higher level around emerging health issues.

The findings also pointed to the importance of engaging health service providers and managers in these processes because, if they were not involved, disputes with and resistance to the health committees could arise. It was necessary to understand local healthcare providers' views, their environment, their needs, and the demands they faced from higher structures. This understanding could help community structures to support healthcare providers in challenging management to better address community needs.

At the same time, health committees needed to be credible in the eyes of the communities they represented by being accountable through regular engagement with community members and by including representatives from diverse groups, especially the most vulnerable.

Health committees working on their own were less able to sustainably address underlying systemic causes of poor health such as poverty, gender, and social destabilization. Collaborating with other civil society organizations could increase their effectiveness as exemplified by the issue of water supply in Uganda. The Cape Town Learning Network also worked with civil society organizations to develop plans for **community** systems-strengthening to address the many underlying social problems.

The overall finding was that for sustainable community engagement, governments need to recognize and incorporate health committees into their health systems in ways that maintain their roles as autonomous agents. In other words, learning to build effective working relations across all key stakeholders is a critical element of health systems and of advancing good health.

In East, Central, and Southern Africa:
Building regional accountability

EQUINET[97] is a membership organization of professionals, researchers, and activists working on health equity across Eastern and Southern Africa. Among their policy-relevant research initiatives has been the production and publication of *Equity Watch* reports in several countries. These country reports, framed by EQUINET, are embedded in policy processes with officials of Ministries of Health and other relevant ministries, to monitor health system progress and responsiveness in promoting and achieving equity in health and healthcare. Each report assesses progress against commitments and goals in four major areas, namely: equity in health, household access to the resources for health, equitable health systems, and global justice. Individual country reports have been prepared with officials in Zambia,[98] Zimbabwe,[99] Uganda,[100] Kenya,[101] Tanzania,[102] and Mozambique.[103] Some countries have prepared multiple *Equity Watch* reports, helping them identify trends and report on their progress in improving health outcomes.

The reports fulfill a resolution of the Ministers of Health in the East, Central, and Southern African Health Community[104] to monitor progress in health equity. Country reports were complemented by a regional Equity Watch[105,106] analysis in 2012, covering 16 countries. The report provided regional decision-makers with evidence on how social and economic disparities were undermining the achievement of targets for reproductive, maternal, and child health, despite some promising commitments made. For example, it noted that:

- Nearly one in five deaths under the age of five took place in the poorest households;

- Fertility rates were higher among adolescents in poor, rural households; and

- Children of mothers with the lowest education levels were five times more likely to be undernourished than those with the most educated mothers (EQUINET 2012a, 2012b).

The work has been widely cited and has subsequently been integrated into the East, Central, and Southern African Health Community's monitoring and evaluation framework to include equity indicators for country reporting.

Accountabilities at the global level

As we noted earlier, governments have been constrained in their choices by global policies and practices that affect financing decisions and implementation priorities. Between 2012 and 2014, EQUINET developed three case studies[107] to explore issues that directly affect the ability of governments to provide quality healthcare services, particularly to vulnerable groups including women, children, and adolescents. The case studies examined the influence of global health governance on health system financing,[108] bottlenecks to local medicine production,[109] and health worker migration from the Global South to the high income countries.[110]

The overall study demonstrated the need for broad multi-stakeholder engagement beyond the health sector to address these key issues. For example, the evidence about African engagement in **global-level** agenda setting, policy development, policy selection and negotiation, and implementation underlined the complexity and political nature of the processes. Governments engaged effectively when there was political leadership with clearly articulated policy positions. It was important to have strong regional interaction and common positions across countries combined with good communication between national sectors and with national embassies and international allies. Negotiators needed to understand the issues and have access to relevant evidence.

At the same time, there was a powerful "development aid" paradigm that weakened the role of a variety of stakeholders including technical actors, the domestic private sector and civil society. International frameworks and the "remoteness of global decision making processes" also weakened abilities to negotiate effectively. Concerns were raised about the impact of development aid focusing on remedial, humanitarian aid related to health rather than looking at the structural factors raised in the case studies. Instead, researchers recommended that new forms of engagement, including South-South cooperation, could be explored. The researchers concluded that to prevent global health diplomacy processes from reverting into "traditional power relationships within a development aid paradigm" it would be necessary to continually examine the institutions, processes, and relationships involved in health diplomacy. Methodologies such as PAR could be very useful in this process (Irwin and Loewenson 2015: 3).

This research has underlined the complexity of factors affecting a government's ability to provide quality services, including reproductive, maternal, and child health services to vulnerable populations. Unless these broader global factors are addressed, services could be siloed, donor-dependent, and unsustainable.

Building trust, creating space for engagement

At the core of governance and as noted in the earlier examples, an important part of negotiating and bringing about change is awareness, understanding, and engagement with the political process. Otherwise, informative evidence might not be used in policy development and implementation. Importantly, however, influencing the policy and decision-making process is not a straight-line process; conflicting interests, power, and competing priorities usually play a significant role in decisions and resource allocation. Simply presenting policy briefs with summarized evidence is unlikely to bring about change. Fundamental to encouraging change is that researchers build trust across health sector actors, including community users, health providers, and decision-makers at all levels. This, however, does not happen automatically.

The issue of building trust and relationships is increasingly recognized as a key factor in challenging unequal power relationships and in influencing change.

Writing in the *BMC Health Services Research* journal,[111] LASDEL's Olivier de Sardan (2015) reflected on the experience of engaging with decision-makers about earlier research into subsidies and fee exemptions. Government officials in Niger initially reacted with reluctance, criticism, and skepticism about LASDEL's evidence on the shortcomings of the policies. LASDEL researchers continued to build the relationships of openness and trust. They believed their role was to "collect the private speak and transmit it to the public sphere through their analyses in order to provide a serious account of a reality" as well as to create "the conditions for an expert debate and a public debate." (Olivier de Sardan 2015: 1). A landmark national conference on fee exemption was held towards the end of project and was deemed a great success. Attended by stakeholders from across the health system, it enabled health workers to speak "for the first time in a public setting about the numerous problems associated with the fee exemption policy, and they largely confirmed and even supplemented the results" of the research.

CHESAI,[112] an initiative supported through UCT and University of Western Cape, deliberately created the space for information sharing and dialogue between researchers, practitioners, and decision-makers in South Africa's Western Cape Province. Monthly journal clubs brought together up to 100 people at a time, including researchers, senior practitioners, and leadership in the provincial health department. The club created the space to reflect, think in new ways, engage with colleagues in a non-threatening setting, and review research results to discuss their implication for local policy and practice. During the evaluations, many members spoke about the need for such fora and the value of bridging the divides that separate these key actors. They also noted that the journal club debates had directly informed the development of provincial health policies.

These examples exemplify the vision of researchers supported by IDRC over the years. It's really what governance for equity in health systems is all about.

A fitting final reflection is shared by Dr Irene Agyepong[113] of the Ghana Health Service:

We need skills in diplomacy, how to mobilise funds and how to sell ideas. Research to policy and practice is not just a once-off dissemination workshop. It is more a question of engaging in the discourse – which importantly means listening, observing, talking with. There are country-to-country and issue-to issue basics that need to be understood; thus context matters. Researchers need to participate in meetings and know their health sector in order to know the major concerns raised in the meetings. This engagement will help to identify research questions and will strengthen the process of transforming research into policy and practice. A critical factor is building relationships with the many different actors – there is need to build trust, credibility, responsiveness so that as the researcher is engaged in policy making, decision-makers may be more likely to listen. This kind of engagement requires different skills sets.

Part 4

Lessons learned and looking forward

This book has presented evidence generated over almost 15 years about how to improve equity, governance, and health systems so that they work more effectively for vulnerable groups such as women, children, and adolescents. We have also distilled lessons from research and experience supported across the globe (see Figure 3) so that it may inform and inspire a new generation of health leaders and researchers, while sharing with others in the global health community, including funding organizations, some critical reflections on the challenges that remain.

Figure 3. The interactive web of lessons to improve equity, governance, and health systems.

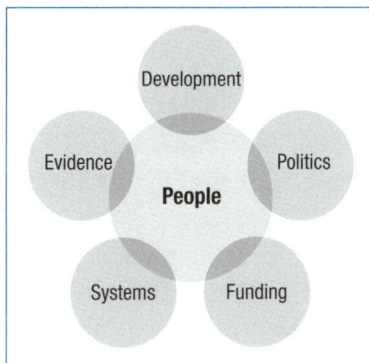

Source: Author

The evidence in this book suggests six overarching lessons about development, people, politics, systems, evidence, and funding. They all matter – both in their own right and through their interactions as an integrated web of influence.

Development matters

Improving health outcomes for women, children, and adolescents is essentially a development challenge.

Research has built the evidence – for example, through the social determinants of health knowledge network NEHSI in Nigeria, INSTRUCT in Botswana, in rural communities in India's Karnataka State, and indigenous communities in Guatemala – demonstrating that many of the root causes of poor health are related to broader factors such as gender attitudes and roles, poverty, lack of education, ethnicity, race, and social marginalization. As noted in Part 1, the early pregnancies associated with a high proportion of preventable maternal and child deaths are rooted in poverty and gendered social practices such as early marriage, violence against women, and lower education levels for girls. Unless such attributes of exclusion are addressed, efforts to improve health will inevitably focus on the symptoms – and the numbers denied good health will continue to grow.

Working on the root causes of poor health, with those whose lives are directly affected, is a long-term process that demands confronting entrenched disparities to achieve lasting impacts for people and institutions. Returning to the tragic death of Sylvia Nalubowa in Uganda, no simple birthing kit was going to address the causes of her death. She was failed at all levels by a system that continued to seek quick fixes for maternal and child mortality – such as establishing emergency obstetric services and distributing birthing kits to expectant mothers. These interventions are at the proximate end of the health system – trying to respond to the immediate symptoms. A development approach focuses at the distal end (Sen and Iyer 2012; Sen, Iyer, and Mukherjee 2009), addressing root causes in vulnerable communities and in dysfunctional systems. The evidence is accumulating on how to prevent needless deaths in childbirth through addressing the underlying causes and drivers of poor health – for example, improving antenatal care in Karnataka, India, including regular testing and treatment of endemic anemia and hypertension; mobilizing community support for pregnant women in India and Nigeria; reorienting all development programs in Botswana so they are accessible to those most vulnerable to HIV infection; and strengthening governance in Ugandan communities so that local health committees could negotiate deployment of additional health staff to village clinics.

Finding sustainable solutions demands providing support and accompanying processes over time: change is a step-by-step, cumulative process and not a series of siloed, one-off interventions.

People matter

Improving health outcomes cannot happen without the full engagement of all those who have a role to play in bringing about change. Responsibilities start at the household and individual level and extend through the community, district, national, regional, and global levels. As EQUINET has shown in East and Southern Africa, it means putting community members, particularly the vulnerable, at the centre of processes to play active roles as engaged citizens. It means understanding the challenges confronting local health providers and working with them to seek the support needed to fully provide quality services. It means working with decision-makers, as the NEHSI team did with state and local authorities in Nigeria, so that they learn how to use evidence, and working with advocates so they know how to use windows of opportunity, and how to lead complex change.

Thought leaders building the field of health systems research are increasingly exploring strategies for strengthening people-centred health systems[114] and have shared their reflections and evidence in a journal supplement supported by IDRC.

Politics matter

Health is political: the quality of service, the extent of access, and the equity provided depends on who is driving the process. Who is deciding for whom? How are decisions made? How is power exercised? This extends to the global level and to funding countries: what development and funding agendas are being set? By whom? In whose interest?

Recent national elections around the world have made this point clear. Health has been used by politicians to win votes and yet, once in power, many begin to undermine people's right to health. Recognizing the political nature of health shapes solutions that address the underlying inequities.

IDRC-funded researchers have worked from community to global levels to address the issues of politics and power that impede equitable health systems. Researchers in rural Uganda and in Cape Town strengthened community citizen engagement to effectively demand services and influence policy. Researchers in Niger became advocates to take on the Ministry of Health and put challenges around implementation of health subsidies on the national agenda. EQUINET research documented the power at play in global health that dramatically affects provision of drugs, health workers, and funding for national health services. Health financing researchers have worked within countries (India); at regional levels in Asia, Africa, and Latin America; and at the global level (GNHE) to document the catastrophic and impoverishing effect of health fees. They also worked to ensure that equitable indicators for UHC were integrated into the SDG monitoring framework. Understanding the power and politics shaped their strategies for engagement.

Systems matter

Health systems must be understood and addressed as a whole. Addressing individual components – whether supply chains, finance, health information systems, or health workers – or individual diseases, services, or population groups in isolation will only serve to further fragment efforts. In Part 1, we looked at how national and global agendas have tended to serially prioritize siloed issues such as HIV/AIDS treatment and immunization, which inevitably directed resources towards the prioritized interventions and diverted them away from the needs of the overall system. The importance has been underlined of continuously putting vulnerable women, children, and adolescents at the centre of UHC policy development and implementation rather than sidelining them in silos in order to ensure that their specific needs are met. And, as was recognized during the Ebola outbreak, it is important to leverage opportunities and resources to integrate these individual priorities into investments that strengthen the overall system to prevent and manage health emergencies.[115]

Evidence matters

Rigorous methodologies are needed to generate reliable data and evidence to inform changes in practice and policy. Of greatest importance are methodologies that analyze exclusion and equity and that can generate actionable findings. Relevant methodologies depend on the research question – as we discussed in Part 3, randomized controlled trials have helped to build the evidence base around the drivers of HIV/AIDS in Southern Africa. Qualitative and participatory research methods, such as those applied in Karnataka, India, in West Africa, and in Guatemala have been essential to digging below the surface and bringing to light the perspectives of those who are not usually heard as well as to expose the invisible workings of power and exclusion. Implementation research, as was undertaken in Bauchi and Cross River States in Nigeria for example, has enabled stakeholders to "learn by doing" and to figure out what works in a specific context.

Equally important is to identify whose questions are being answered. If research is not driven by the needs of communities and stakeholders seeking to inform themselves and drive change, it is unlikely to be relevant. These methodologies enable stakeholder groups to take ownership of research and use it as a basis for action.

To be useful, evidence must be shared back with all stakeholders in forms that can be used. Formats will differ according to specific stakeholder roles and responsibilities. It is crucial that the analysis and interpretation of data involve those who will use the evidence to encourage change: linear processes whereby researchers pursue answers to their own questions and present solutions only through policy briefs are insufficient and ineffective in trying to address complex and entrenched health problems.

Funding matters

As reflected in the SDGs, and underscored by the extensive work of the health finance researchers, there is growing consensus about the importance of UHC as a strategy for providing accessible, quality and affordable care. Methodologies have been developed to improve the analysis of national financing mechanisms and efforts to implement UHC. Part 3 presented evidence from efforts to implement health insurance schemes in India, Ghana, Tanzania, and South Africa. The current HIV/AIDS research in Botswana is supporting the government to re-orient its own national programs to ensure they are accessible to vulnerable adolescent girls and young women.

At the same time, the research has shown the ongoing influence of donor agendas and priorities on national strategies and resource allocation as we saw around the imposition and subsequent selected abolition of fees for health services across West Africa. More recently, researchers writing about efforts to strengthen health systems in West Africa[116] point to the continued skewing effects of development assistance that divert efforts to externally determined priorities.

Given this powerful role of international aid and assistance in the global health arena, some of the following reflections and lessons emerging from IDRC's work may be of interest and relevance.

First and foremost, we need to listen and put LMIC stakeholders and researchers, and their knowledge, at the centre of research and development processes. Those grounded in the relevant social, political, and economic contexts need to lead the research and use the findings to promote sustainable change. Funders can play an important role by enabling the space for creativity, vision, and relationship-building rather than forcing prescriptive approaches and subsequently trying to ensure buy-in. Providing shorter initial planning grants can help key actors bridge linguistic, disciplinary, and other divides and build the needed relationships of trust to develop sound contextually relevant research proposals. Building in support to enable ongoing dialogue and reflection across stakeholder groups can contribute to the identification of relevant research questions and to the development of strategies to inform policy and practice.

Change does not happen overnight and we need to provide long-term windows of support through multiple-year funding. The metrics of success are also important. Does it make sense to focus on broad indicators such as a reduction in MMRs? Much debate took place around this particular MDG indicator (Yamin and Boulanger 2014), with scientists arguing that it was not feasible or realistic to measure or attain. What are the important intermediate steps that need to happen to contribute to such a broad change and how can they be measured? As we have noted, equity and governance are about power relations and who controls resources and decision-making at all levels. How can changes and progress in these aspects be made visible and measured?

Part 5

Looking forward: Seizing a window of opportunity

Women, children, and adolescents constitute some of the most vulnerable groups in the majority of societies. Globally, there are numerous efforts underway to strengthen health systems and to improve reproductive, maternal, and child health. As repeatedly noted in the book, however, focusing only on one population group or only on narrow medical needs around pregnancy and childbirth is not sufficient to sustainably improve people's lives. Too often, the organizations and individuals involved remain in separate silos and it is important to bridge the divides that fragment efforts. It is critical to support comprehensive approaches that address the structural drivers of poor health and strengthen health systems for all vulnerable groups, including women, children, and adolescents.

Until 2030, the SDGs provide a strategic window of opportunity for advancing health outcomes. Goal number three on health and well-being adopts a life-course approach that puts the emphasis on reproductive, women's, children's, and adolescents' health.

It integrates knowledge and evidence about the social determinants of health and calls for integrated, holistic, multi-sectoral responses. It calls for UHC to ensure both access to quality services for all as well as provision of financial protection to prevent catastrophic expenses that propel families into deeper poverty.

Supporting the development of relevant methodologies, the generation and use of rigorous evidence, and stakeholder engagement to build understanding and consensus around national priorities will help to advance this goal and strengthen the decision-making, resource allocation, and governance needed to follow through on commitments.

Such comprehensive efforts will strengthen the systems that can deliver improved reproductive, women's, children's, and adolescent health as well as contribute to prevention and any needed management of future health emergencies such as the Ebola virus outbreak. This may be one silver lining to the tragic Ebola outbreak – it dramatically demonstrated the level of increased global interdependence and helped to build global consensus and mobilization around the need to support holistic, integrated approaches to address entrenched health and development problems. It graphically illustrated that we need to understand the politics and context of poor health; address the proximate and distal causes of poor health; and build bridges across siloed, vertical interventions and fragmented stakeholder groups in order to build strong equitable health systems.

While the SDGs provide a strong global framework for action, we must guard against complacency, drawing on lessons from our wealth of collective experience. The words of Amartya Sen, written in 2004, are as relevant today as they were over a decade ago:

The global health crisis we face today demands fresh reflection and new departures. Central to this encounter is the development and use of social and scientific knowledge. The crisis does, of course, demand dedicated action as well as faith in humankind's ability to overcome monumental adversities. But we need a knowledge-centred approach to make our actions fit the needs ... (Ahrweiler, H. et al. 2004:38)[117]

Glossary of terms and abbreviations

CEHURD – Center for Health, Human Rights and Development

CHESAI – Collaboration for Health Systems Analysis and Innovation

EQUINET – Regional Network on Equity in Health in East and Southern Africa

EQUITAP – Equity in Asia-Pacific Health Systems

EU – European Union

GHIs – Global Health Initiatives

GNHE – Global Network for Health Equity

IDRC – International Development Research Centre

IHRs – International Health Regulations

IIMB – Indian Institute of Management Bangalore

INSTRUCT – Inter-ministerial National Structural Intervention Trial

KT – knowledge translation

LAnet-EHS – Latin American Research Network on Equity and Health Systems

LASDEL – Laboratoire d'études et de recherches sur les dynamiques sociales et le développement local

LGA – Local Government Area

LMICs – low- and middle-income countries

MDGs – Millennium Development Goals

MDR – maternal death review

MMR – maternal mortality ratio

MNCH – maternal, newborn, and child health

NEHSI - Nigeria Evidence-based Health System Initiative

NGOs – non-governmental organizations

PAR – participatory action research

PHC – primary healthcare

PHFI – Public Health Foundation of India

SDGs – Sustainable Development Goals

SHIELD – Strategies for Health Insurance for Equity in Less Developed Countries

SRH – Sexual and reproductive health

SRHR – Sexual and reproductive health and rights

SSA – sub-Saharan Africa

UCT – University of Cape Town's School of Public Health and Family Medicine

UHC – universal health coverage

WHO – World Health Organization

Endnotes

1 http://www.who.int/topics/international_health_regulations/en/ [Accessed May 9, 2017].

2 http://www.unfpa.org/events/international-conference-population-and-development-icpd [Accessed May 9, 2017].

3 http://www.unfpa.org/sites/default/files/event-pdf/PoA_en.pdf [Accessed May 9, 2017].

4 http://www.un.org/millenniumgoals/ [Accessed May 9, 2017].

5 http://www.un.org/sustainabledevelopment/sustainable-development-goals/ [Accessed May 9, 2017].

6 The ebook can be found at www.idrc.ca/healthy-lives. We do recognize that links can change over time; however, we hope the information provides sufficient detail to track down the references as needed.

7 http://www.cehurd.org/wp-content/uploads/downloads/2015/11/Press-Release-Maternal-Health-Uganda.pdf [Accessed May 9, 2017].

8 http://www.un.org/millenniumgoals/ [Accessed May 9, 2017].

9 Specifically, Goal 4 was to reduce the under-five mortality rate by two-thirds between 1990 and 2015, and Goal 5 was to a) reduce the maternal mortality ratio by three quarters between 1990 and 2015, and b) to achieve universal access to reproductive health by 2015. (Source: UN millennium goals: http://www.un.org/millenniumgoals/) [Accessed May 9, 2017].

10 http://www.un.org/sustainabledevelopment/sustainable-development-goals/ [Accessed May 9, 2017].

11 http://www.who.int/life-course/partners/global-strategy/global-strategy-2016-2030/en/ [Accessed May 9, 2017].

12 http://www.un.org/sustainabledevelopment/health/ [Accessed May 9, 2017].

13 http://www.prb.org/pdf16/prb-wpds2016-web-2016.pdf [Accessed May 9, 2017].

14 Abridged from Annex 7 of WHO et al. 2015: *Trends in maternal mortality* (MMR, maternal deaths per 100 000 live births), number of maternal deaths, lifetime risk, percentage of AIDS-related indirect maternal deaths and proportion of deaths among women of reproductive age that are due to maternal causes (PM), by country, 2015.

15 Excerpts from Annex 7 table. Note: Estimates have been computed to ensure comparability across countries, thus they are not necessarily the same as official statistics of the countries, which may use alternative rigorous methods.

16 http://www.who.int/social_determinants/thecommission/finalreport/key_concepts/en/ [Accessed May 9, 2017].

17 http://www.who.int/social_determinants/resources/csdh_media/hskn_final_2007_en.pdf [Accessed May 9, 2017].

18 http://apps.who.int/iris/bitstream/10665/43943/1/9789241563703_eng.pdf [Accessed May 9, 2017].

19 http://www.who.int/social_determinants/en/ [Accessed May 9, 2017].

20 http://www.who.int/social_determinants/en/ [Accessed May 9, 2017].

21 http://www.who.int/publications/almaata_declaration_en.pdf [Accessed May 9, 2017].

22 http://www.who.int/whr/2008/en/ [Accessed May 9, 2017].

23 http://www.who.int/whr/2000/en/ [Accessed May 9, 2017].

24 Full supplement can be found at https://bmcinthealthhumrights.biomedcentral.com/articles/supplements/volume-9-supplement-1 [Accessed May 9, 2017].

25 http://www.who.int/healthsystems/publications/MPS_academic_case_studies_Book_01.pdf [Accessed May 9, 2017].

26 http://data.worldbank.org/indicator/SH.STA.MMRT?locations=UG [Accessed May 9, 2017].

27 http://www.un.org/ga/aids/pdf/abuja_declaration.pdf [Accessed May 9, 2017]. (NOTE: This page will only open if you manually add the link to your browser.)

28 http://www.actionforglobalhealth.eu/fileadmin/AfGH_Intranet/AFGH/Publications/PolicyBriefing1_Final1_LoRes.pdf [Accessed May 9, 2017].

29 http://www.wpro.who.int/laos/topics/universal_health_coverage/en/ [Accessed May 9, 2017].

30 http://www.who.int/health_financing/universal_coverage_definition/en/ [Accessed May 9, 2017].

31 http://www.who.int/whr/en/ [Accessed May 9, 2017].

32 http://universalhealthcoverageday.org/welcome/ [Accessed May 9, 2017].

33 https://sustainabledevelopment.un.org/sdg3 [Accessed May 9, 2017].

34 Phase 2 of IDRC's Governance, Equity, and Health program (2006-2011) supported 97 projects with CA$ 21.5 million in funding from IDRC and a further CA$ 54.84 million from seven donor partners. (Source: Singh et al. 2010) Phase 3 (2011-2016) supported 68 projects with a total of CA$ 95.3 million, including CA$ 36.2 million of external donor funds (Source: IDRC 2015).

35 https://www.idrc.ca/sites/default/files/sp/ Documents%20EN /GEHS-Maternal-Health.pdf [Accessed May 9, 2017].

36 Laboratoire d'étude et de recherches sur les dynamiques sociales et le développement local (LASDEL) http://www.lasdel.net/ [Accessed May 9, 2017].

37 http://www.equinetafrica.org/sites/default/files/uploads/ documents/PAR%20Methods%20Reader2014%20for%20web.pdf [Accessed May 9, 2017].

38 Global Network for Health Equity http://gnhe.org/blog/ [Accessed May 9, 2017].

39 CIET. http://instruct.cietresearch.org/ [Accessed May 9, 2017].

40 http://www.issp.bf/; https://www.idrc.ca/en/project/ building-capacity-health-systems-and-policy-analysis- sub-saharan-africa [Accessed May 9, 2017].

41 https://www.idrc.ca/en/article/boosting-capacity-health- research-africa [Accessed May 9, 2017].

42 http://www.chesai.org/ [Accessed May 9, 2017].

43 http://www.sochara.org/ [Accessed May 9, 2017].

44 http://www.comcahpss.org/2017/01/12/welcome-to-comcahpss/ [Accessed May 9, 2017].

45 Using evidence to strengthen health systems in Africa and the Middle East (project profile). https://www.idrc.ca/en/project/using-evidence-strengthen-health-systems-africa-and-middle-east [Accessed May 9, 2017].

46 http://iimb.ac.in/ [Accessed May 9, 2017] (NOTE: This page will only open if you manually add the link to your browser.)

47 http://cietresearch.org/ [Accessed May 9, 2017].

48 http://instruct.cietresearch.org/choice-disability/ [Accessed May 9, 2017].

49 Summaries: https://www.idrc.ca/en/project/reducing-hiv-risk-botswana-national-cluster-randomized-controlled-trial [Accessed May 9, 2017]; http://instruct.cietresearch.org/trial-design/ [Accessed May 9, 2017].

50 http://instruct.cietresearch.org/trial-design/ [Accessed May 9, 2017].

51 http://hiv.cietresearch.org/choice-disability-interventions/beyond-victims-and-villains/ [Accessed May 9, 2017].

52 https://www.idrc.ca/en/article/using-evidence-reduce-maternal-deaths-nigeria [Accessed May 9, 2017].

53 http://nigeria.cietresearch.org/ [Accessed May 9, 2017].

54 http://www.ciet.org/en/project/nigeria-a-health-information-and-planning-system-for-bauchi-and/ [Accessed May 9, 2017].

55 The CIET methods documentary provides a step-by-step overview of the process. Information on the full NEHSI implementation is available on the CIET website, highlighting the first cycle focusing on maternal health and the second cycle on child health [Accessed May 9, 2017].

56 http://www.ciet.org/en/theme/social-audits/ [Accessed May 9, 2017].

57 CIET video on NEHSI social audit https://www.youtube.com/watch?v=0CyYa8eJNww [Accessed May 9, 2017].

58 http://nigeria.cietresearch.org/social-audits/demo-social-audit/ [Accessed May 9, 2017].

59 http://www.ciet.org/en/method/sepa-communication/ [Accessed May 9, 2017].

60 See: https://www.youtube.com/watch?v=ahHpwqhndg8; https://www.youtube.com/watch?v=bdvN-mId058; https://www.youtube.com/watch?v=clieIk88I9I [Accessed May 9, 2017]. For additional videos, search NEHSI videos on www.youtube.com.

61 http://nigeria.cietresearch.org/most-significant-change/ [Accessed May 9, 2017].

62 More information on the methods documentary https://www.youtube.com/watch?v=0CyYa8eJNww [Accessed May 9, 2017].

63 https://www.idrc.ca/sites/default/files/sp/ Documents%20EN/NEHSI-process-document.pdf [Accessed May 9, 2017].

64 https://www.unicef.org/sowc08/docs/sowc08_panel_2_5.pdf [Accessed May 9, 2017].

65 http://www.lasdel.net/ [Accessed May 9, 2017].

66 Recent findings on user fee exemption policies in Burkina Faso, Mali, and Niger can be found in a peer-reviewed 2016 special supplement of the *BMC Health Services Research* journal (Volume 15, supplement 3) available at https://bmchealthservres.biomedcentral.com/articles/supplements/volume-15-supplement-3 [Accessed May 9, 2017].

67 Percentage change in MMR is based on rounded numbers. (WHO et al. 2015: 77).

68 Progress towards MDG 5A (i.e., to reduce MMR by 75% between 1990 and 2015) was assessed for the 95 countries with an MMR higher than 100 in 1990. See section 4.1 and Box 5 for additional details in the full report: World Health Organization (WHO), United Nations Children's Fund (UNICEF), United Nations Population Fund (UNFPA), World Bank Group, United Nations Population Division (UNPD). Trends in maternal mortality: 1990 to 2015. Geneva: WHO; 2015 (available from: http://www.who.int/reproductivehealth/publications/monitoring/maternal-mortality-2015/en/). (WHO et al. 2015: 77) [Accessed May 9, 2017].

69 https://www.youtube.com/watch?v=UIr_EJM7JbQ [Accessed May 9, 2017].

70 For more info visit website http://uhc-india.org/index.php including the final report of the High Level Group. [Accessed May 9, 2017].

71 For more information: https://www.idrc.ca/en/project/preparing-states-india-universal-health-coverage-0 [Accessed May 9, 2017].

72 http://www.phfi.org/images/home/essential_health_package_ for_india.pdf [Accessed May 9, 2017].

73 http://www.equitap.org/ [Accessed May 9, 2017].

74 https://www.idrc.ca/en/book/financing-health-latin-america-
household-spending-and-impoverishment
[Accessed September 22, 2017].

75 https://academic.oup.com/heapol/issue/27/suppl_1
[Accessed May 9, 2017].

76 http://gnhe.org/blog/ [Accessed May 9, 2017].

77 http://gnhe.org/blog/2016/01/01/measuring-progress-
towards-uhc/ [Accessed May 9, 2017].

78 Universal coverage is generally seen as comprising three
dimensions: proportion of the population covered, the
proportion of health services covered, and the degree of
financial risk protection. Source: WHO http://www.who.int/
health_financing/strategy/dimensions/en/
[Accessed May 9, 2017].

79 http://gnhe.org/blog/2015/05/11/gnhes-consensus-
statement-on-universal-health-coverage-2/
[Accessed May 9, 2017].

80 Target 3.8 Achieve universal health coverage, including
financial risk protection, access to quality essential health-care
services and access to safe, effective, quality and affordable
essential medicines and vaccines for all
http://www.un.org/sustainabledevelopment/health/
[Accessed May 9, 2017].

81 https://unstats.un.org/unsd/statcom/48th-session/
[Accessed May 9, 2017].

82 https://www.uhc2030.org/news-events/uhc2030-news/
article/uhc-indicators-for-sdg-monitoring-framework-
agreed-398330/ [Accessed September 22, 2017].

83 http://gnhe.org/blog/uhc-assessments/ [Accessed May 9, 2017].

84 http://gnhe.org/blog/uhc-assessments/ [Accessed May 9, 2017].

85 http://unsdsn.org/ [Accessed May 9, 2017].

86 http://idris.idrc.ca/app/Search?request=directAccess& projectNumber=107399&language=en [Accessed May 9, 2017].

87 http://unsdsn.org/wp-content/uploads/2014/02/Health-For-All-Report.pdf [Accessed May 9, 2017].

88 https://www.idrc.ca/en/project/fair-path-toward-universal-coverage-national-case-study-ethiopia-uganda-and-zambia [Accessed May 9, 2017].

89 http://www.who.int/choice/documents/making_fair_ choices /en/ [Accessed May 9, 2017].

90 http://www.tandfonline.com/toc/rgph20/10/2 [Accessed May 9, 2017].

91 http://cegss.org.gt/ [Accessed May 9, 2017].

92 https://www.idrc.ca/en/project/enhancing-participation-indigenous-people-address-discrimination-and-promote-equity-health [Accessed May 9, 2017].

93 A short documentary video (http://www.copasah.net/centro-de-estudios-para-la-equidad-y-gobernanza-en-los-sistemas-de-salud.html) describes the strategy and process that they have followed. [Accessed May 9, 2017].

94 http://www.cehurd.org/ [Accessed May 9, 2017].

95 http://www.publichealth.uct.ac.za/ [Accessed May 9, 2017].

[96] http://salearningnetwork.weebly.com/ [Accessed May 9, 2017].

[97] https://www.equinetafrica.org/ [Accessed May 9, 2017].

[98] http://www.equinetafrica.org/sites/default/files/uploads/documents/Zambia_EW_Aug_2011_web.pdf [Accessed May 9, 2017].

[99] http://www.equinetafrica.org/sites/default/files/uploads/documents/Zimbabwe_EW_2014.pdf [Accessed May 9, 2017].

[100] http://www.equinetafrica.org/sites/default/files/uploads/documents/Uganda_EW_Nov2011_lfs.pdf [Accessed May 9, 2017].

[101] http://www.equinetafrica.org/sites/default/files/uploads/documents/Kenya_EW_Dec2011_lfs.pdf [Accessed May 9, 2017].

[102] http://www.equinetafrica.org/sites/default/files/uploads/documents/Tanzania_EW_January2013.pdf [Accessed May 9, 2017].

[103] http://www.equinetafrica.org/sites/default/files/uploads/documents/Moz_EW_Eng_Oct2010.pdf [Accessed May 9, 2017].

[104] http://www.ecsahc.org/ [Accessed May 9, 2017].

[105] http://www.equinetafrica.org/sites/default/files/uploads/documents/Regional_EW_2012_Part_2w.pdf [Accessed May 9, 2017].

[106] http://www.equinetafrica.org/sites/default/files/uploads/documents/Regional_EW_2012_Part_1w.pdf [Accessed May 9, 2017].

[107] Published in a special issue of the *Journal of Health Diplomacy* [Accessed May 9, 2017].

108 http://www.equinetafrica.org/sites/default/files/uploads/
documents/GHD%20Gov%20Diss%20Paper%20102.pdf
[Accessed May 9, 2017].

109 http://www.equinetafrica.org/sites/default/files/uploads/
documents/GHD_Meds_Diss_Paper_104.pdf
[Accessed May 9, 2017].

110 http://www.equinetafrica.org/sites/default/files/uploads/
doc uments/GHD%20Code%20Final%20rep%20Diss103%
20June2014.pdf [Accessed May 9, 2017].

111 http://bmchealthservres.biomedcentral.com/articles/
10.11 86/1472-6963-15-S3-S4 [Accessed May 9, 2017].

112 http://www.chesai.org/ [Accessed May 9, 2017].

113 Comment during a proposal development workshop hosted
by the West African Health Organisation, Bobo-Dioulasso,
Burkina Faso, October 2012.

114 https://academic.oup.com/heapol/issue/29/suppl_2
[Accessed May 9, 2017].

115 For more on this, read *Health Policy and Planning*'s 2012
Special Supplement on Systems thinking for health systems
strengthening in LMICs: Seizing the opportunity.
http://www.who.int/alliance-hpsr/resources/hppsupplement
systemsthinking/en/ [Accessed May 9, 2017].

116 People and research: improved health systems for West
Africans by West Africans (2017). *Health Research Policy and
Systems* (Volume 15, supplement 1). https://health-policy-
systems.biomedcentral.com/articles/supplements/volume-15-
supplement-1 [Accessed July 21, 2017].

117 http://institut.veolia.org/sites/g/files/dvc1121/f/assets/
documents/2016/08/Knowledge_systems_for_sustainable_
development.pdf [Accessed May 9, 2017].

Sources and resources

Aberese Ako, M.; van Djik, H.; Gerrits, T.; Arhinful, D.K.; Agyepong, I.A. (2014). "Your health our concern, our health whose concern?": Perceptions of injustice in organizational relationships and processes and frontline health worker motivation in Ghana. *Health Policy and Planning*, 29(Suppl 2): ii15-ii28. DOI: https://doi.org/10.1093/heapol/czu068 [Accessed May 15, 2017].

Action for Global Health and DSW (2010). *Health Spending in Uganda: The impact of current aid structures and aid effectiveness.* http://www.actionforglobalhealth.eu/fileadmin/AfGH_Intranet/ AFGH/Publications/PolicyBriefing1_Final1_LoRes.pdf [Accessed May 15, 2017].

Ahrweiler, H.; Caplan, K.; Charpak, G. et al. (2004). *Knowledge Systems for Sustainable Development.* Paris: Institut Veolia Environ-nement and Institut Pasteur. http://institut.veolia.org/sites/g/ files/dvc1121/f/assets/documents/2016/08/Knowledge_systems_ for_sustainable_development.pdf [Accessed May 15, 2017].

Andersson, N. (2011a). Building the community voice into planning: 25 years of methods development in social audit. *BMC Health Services Research 2011*, 11(Suppl 2): S1. http://www.biomedcentral.com/1472-6963/11/S2/S1 [Accessed April 10, 2017].

Andersson, N. (2011b). Proof of impact and pipeline planning: directions and challenges for social audit in the health sector. *BMC Health Services Research 2011*, 11(Suppl 2): S16. http://www.biomedcentral.com/1472-6963/11/S2/S16 [Accessed April 10, 2017].

Andersson, N.; Omer, K.; Caldwell, D.; Dambam, M.M.; Miakudi, A.Y.; Effiong, B.; Ikpi, E.; Udofia, E.; Khan, A.; Ansari, U.; Ansari, N.; Hamel, C. (2011). Male responsibility and maternal morbidity: a cross-sectional study in two Nigerian states. *BMC Health Services Research 2011*, 11(Suppl 2): S7. http://www.biomedcentral.com/1472-6963/11/S2/S7 [Accessed April 10, 2017].

Andersson, N.; Cockcroft, A. (2012). Choice-Disability and HIV Infection: A Cross Sectional Study of HIV Status in Botswana, Namibia and Swaziland. *AIDS Behav*, 16: 189-198. DOI: 10.1007/s10461-011-9912-3. https://www.ncbi.nlm.nih.gov/pmc/articles/PMC3254870/ [Accessed April 10, 2017].

Barbiero, V.K. (2014). It's not Ebola .... It's the systems. *Global Health: Science and Practice*, 2(4): 374-375. http://www.ghspjournal.org/content/2/4/374.full [Accessed April 10, 2017].

Bergkvist, S.; Wagstaff, A.; Katyal, A.; Singh, P.V.; Samarth, A.; Rao, M. (2014). *What a Difference a State Makes: Health Reform in Andhra Pradesh*. Washington: The World Bank. Development Research Group. Human Development and Public Services Team. DOI: http://elibrary.worldbank.org/doi/abs/10.1596/1813-9450-6883 [Accessed April 10, 2017].

Bhatt, P.; Madge,V.; Mor, N.; Singh, A.; Jain, N.; Balasubramaniam, P. (n.d.). *Developing and Costing State-Flexible Essential Health Package (EHP) for India*. New Delhi: PHFI. http://www.phfi.org/images/home/essential_health_package_for_india.pdf [Accessed April 10, 2017].

Brearley, L., Mohamed, S.; Eriyagama, V.; Elwalagedara, R.; Rannan-Eliya, R.P. (2012). *Impact of maternal and child health private expenditure on poverty and inequity: Review of the literature on the extent and mechanisms by which maternal, newborn and child healthcare expenditures exacerbate poverty with focus on evidence from Asia and the Pacific.* Mandaluyong City, Philippines: Asian Development Bank. https://www.adb.org/sites/default/files/publication/30156/impact-maternal-child-health-private-expenditure.pdf [Accessed April 10, 2017].

Carden, F. (2009). *Knowledge to Policy: Making the Most of Development Research.* Ottawa and New Delhi: IDRC and Sage Publications. https://idl-bnc-idrc.dspacedirect.org/handle/10625/37706 [Accessed May 15, 2017].

Center for Health, Human Rights and Development (2011). *Advocating for the Right to Reproductive HealthCare in Uganda: The Import of Constitutional Petition No.16 of 2011.* http://www.cehurd.org/wp-content/uploads/downloads/2012/01/Petition-16-Study.pdf [Accessed April 10, 2017].

Center for Health, Human Rights and Development (2015). Press release, October 30, 2015. http://www.cehurd.org/wp-content/uploads/downloads/2015/11/Press-Release-Maternal-Health-Uganda.pdf [Accessed April 10, 2017].

CIET Trust (2006). *Demonstration social audit (multi stakeholder surveillance): Cross River State 2006.* Summary Report. http://nigeria.cietresearch.org/files/2013/01/demo-audit-cross-river-summary.pdf [Accessed April 10, 2017].

Cockcroft, A.; Usman, M.U.; Nyamucherera, O.F.; Emori, H.; Duke, B.; Umar, N.A.; Andersson, N. (2014). Why children are not vaccinated against measles: A cross-sectional study in two Nigerian States. *Archives of Public Health*, 72: 48. http://www.archpublichealth.com/content/72/1/48 [Accessed May 15, 2017].

Desai, M.; Phillips-Howard, P.A.; Odhiambo, F.O.; Katana, A.; Ouma, P.; Hamel, M.J.; Omoto, J.; Macharia, S.; van Eijk, A.; Ogwang, S.; Slutsker, L.; Laserson, K.F. (2013). An Analysis of Pregnancy-Related Mortality in the KEMRI/CDC Health and Demographic Surveillance System in Western Kenya. *Plos One*, 8(7): e68733. http://journals.plos.org/plosone/article/asset?id=10.1371%2Fjournal.pone.0068733.PDF [Accessed April 10, 2017].

Diarra, A.; Ousseini, A. 2015. The coping strategies of front-line health workers in the context of user fee exemptions in Niger. *BMC Health Services Research 2015*, 15(Suppl 3): S1. http://www.biomedcentral.com/1472-6963/15/S3/S1 [Accessed April 10, 2017].

Dugger, C.W. 2011. Maternal Deaths Focus Harsh Light on Uganda. *The New York Times*, July 29, 2011. http://www.nytimes.com/2011/07/30/world/africa/30uganda.html [Accessed April 10, 2017].

Ekirapa-Kiracho, E.; Namazzi, G.; Tetui, M.; Mutebi, A.; Waiswa, P.; Htet, O.; Peters, D.H.; George, A. (2016). Unlocking community capabilities for improving maternal and newborn health: participatory action research to improve birth preparedness, health facility access, and newborn care in rural Uganda. *BMC Health Services Research 2016*, 16(Suppl 7): 638. DOI: 10.1186/s12913-016-1864-x. https://bmchealthservres.biomedcentral.com/articles/10.1186/s12913-016-1864-x [Accessed April 10, 2017].

EQUINET (2012a). *Regional Equity Watch 2012: Assessing progress towards equity in health - East and Southern Africa.* Harare: EQUINET. http://www.equinetafrica.org/sites/default/files/uploads/documents/Regional_EW_2012_Part_1w.pdf [Accessed April 10, 2017].

EQUINET (2012b). *Challenging inequities through redistributive health systems.* Harare: EQUINET. http://www.equinetafrica.org/sites/default/files/uploads/documents/Regional%20EW%202012%20Part%202w.pdf [Accessed April 10, 2017].

Every Woman Every Child (UN facilitated working group) (2015). *Survive, Thrive, Transform: Global Strategy for Women's, Children's and Adolescents' Health (2016-2030).* http://globalstrategy.everywomaneverychild.org/pdf/EWEC_globalstrategyreport_200915_FINAL_WEB.pdf [Accessed April 10, 2017].

Fan, V.Y.; Karan, A.; Mahal, A. (2012). State health insurance and out-of-pocket health expenditures in Andhra Pradesh, India. *Int J Health Care Finance Econ,* 12(3): 189-215. DOI: 10.1007/s10754-012-9110-5. https://scholar.harvard.edu/vfan/publications/state-health-insurance-and-out-pocket-health-expenditures-andhra-pradesh-india [Accessed April 10, 2017].

Fidler, D.P. (2009). Background paper on Developing a Research Agenda for the Bellagio Meeting #1, 23-26 March 2009. *Globalization, Trade and Health Working Papers Series,* Geneva: WHO.

Flores, W.; Ruano, A.L.; Funchal, D.P. (2009). Social participation within a context of political violence: Implications for the promotion and exercise of the right to health in Guatemala. *Health and Human Rights,* 11(1). https://www.hhrjournal.org/2013/09/social-participation-within-a-context-of-political-violence-implications-for-the-promotion-and-exercise-of-the-right-to-health-in-guatemala/ [Accessed April 10, 2017].

Gates, B. (2015). The next epidemic – lessons from Ebola. *The New England Journal of Medicine,* 372: 1381-1384. DOI: http://www.nejm.org/doi/full/10.1056/NEJMp1502918 [Accessed April 10, 2017].

Germain, A.; Sen, G.; Garcia-Moreno, C.; Shankar, M. (2015). Advancing sexual and reproductive health and rights in low- and middle-income countries: Implications for the post-2015 global development agenda. *Global Public Health*, 10(2): 137-148. https://www.ncbi.nlm.nih.gov/pmc/articles/ PMC4318089/pdf/rgph-10-137.pdf [Accessed May 15, 2017].

Global summit to end sexual violence in conflict (2014). https://www.gov.uk/government/collections/2014-global-summit-to-end-sexual-violence-in-conflict [Accessed May 15, 2017].

Gostin, L.; Friedman, E. (2015). A retrospective and prospective analysis of the west African Ebola virus disease epidemic: robust national health systems at the foundation and an empowered WHO at the apex. *The Lancet*, 385(9980): 1902-1909. http://www.thelancet.com/journals/lancet/article/PIIS0140-6736(15)60644-4/abstract [Accessed April 10, 2017].

Goudge, J.; Akazili, J.; Ataguba, J.; Kuwawenaruwa, A.; Borghi, J.; Harris, B.; Mills, A. (2012). Social solidarity and willingness to tolerate risk- and income-related cross-subsidies within health insurance: experiences from Ghana, Tanzania and South Africa. *Health Policy Plan*, 27(Suppl 1): i55-i63. DOI: https://doi.org/10.1093/heapol/czs008 [Accessed April 10, 2017].

Government of India. Ministry of Health and Family Welfare. National Commission on Macroeconomics and Health (2005). *Report of the National Commission on Macroeconomics and Health.* New Delhi: Ministry. http://www.who.int/macrohealth/action/ Report%20of%20the%20National%20Commission.pdf?ua=1 [Accessed April 10, 2017].

Government of Mozambique. Ministry of Health, TARSC/EQUINET (2010). *Equity Watch 2010: Assessing Progress towards Equity in Health in Mozambique.* Maputo and Harare. http://www.equinetafrica.org/sites/default/files/uploads/ documents/Moz_EW_Eng_Oct2010.pdf [Accessed April 10, 2017].

Government of Nigeria (2013). *Nigeria Millennium Development Goals 2013 Report.* http://www.ng.undp.org/content/dam/

nigeria/docs/MDGs/UNDP_NG_MDGsReport2013.pdf
[Accessed April 10, 2017].

Government of Nigeria (2014). *Building a culture of evidence-based planning: A process document.* The Nigeria evidence-based health system initiative (NEHSI) approach in Bauchi and Cross Rivers States. Ottawa: International Development Research Centre and Foreign Affairs, Trade and Development Canada, Government of Canada. https://idl-bnc-idrc.dspacedirect.org/bitstream/handle/10625/53553/IDL-53553.pdf?sequence=1&isAllowed=y [Accessed April 10, 2017].

Green, A. (2016). West African countries focus on post-Ebola recovery plans. *www.thelancet.com*, 388: 2463-2465. http://www.thelancet.com/journals/lancet/article/PIIS0140-6736(16)32219-X/fulltext?rss%3Dyes [Accessed April 10, 2017].

Heymann, D.L.; Chen, L.; Takemi, K. et al. (2015). Global health security: the wider lessons from the west African Ebola virus disease epidemic. *The Lancet*, 385(9980): 1884-1901. http://www.thelancet.com/journals/lancet/article/PIIS0140-6736(15)60858-3/abstract [Accessed May 15, 2017].

Horton, R. (2014). Offline: The third revolution in global health. *The Lancet*, 383(9929): 1620. DOI: http://dx.doi.org/10.1016/S0140-6736(14)60769-8. http://www.thelancet.com/journals/lancet/article/PIIS0140-6736(14)60769-8/fulltext?rss%3Dyes= [Accessed April 10, 2017].

Ifakara Health Institute, Ministry of Health and Social Welfare, Training and Research Support Centre (2012). *Equity Watch 2012: Assessing progress towards equity in health in Tanzania.* Dar es Salaam and Harare: EQUINET. http://www.equinetafrica.org/ sites/default/files/uploads/documents/Tanzania_EW_January2013.pdf [Accessed April 10, 2017].

Institute for Health Metrics and Evaluation (IHME) (2016). *Financing Global Health 2015: Development assistance steady on the path to new Global Goals.* Seattle, WA: IHME. http://www.healthdata.org/sites/default/files/files/policy_report/ FGH/2016/IHME_PolicyReport_FGH_2015.pdf [Accessed April 10, 2017].

International Center for Research on Women (2016a). Child Marriage Around the World. http://www.icrw.org/child-marriage-facts-and-figures/ [Accessed April 10, 2017].

International Center for Research on Women (2016b). Sexual and Reproductive Health and Rights. https://www.icrw.org/ issues/reproductive-health/ [Accessed May 15, 2017].

International Development Research Centre (2014). Research findings are catalyst to nationwide rollout of HIV prevention program in Botswana. https://www.idrc.ca/en/article/research-findings-are-catalyst-nationwide-rollout-hiv-prevention-program-botswana [Accessed April 10, 2017].

International Development Research Centre (2015). *Final Prospectus Report on Governance for Equity in Health Systems.* Ottawa: IDRC. https://idl-bnc-idrc.dspacedirect.org/handle/ 10625/55338 [Accessed May 15, 2017].

International Development Research Centre (n.d.). Maternal Health: Making Health Systems Work for Mother and Child. Ottawa: IDRC. https://www.idrc.ca/sites/default/files/sp/ Documents%20EN/GEHS-Maternal-Health.pdf [Accessed April 10, 2017].

Irwin, R.; Loewenson, R. (2015). Health diplomacy: perspectives from east and southern Africa. *Journal of Health Diplomacy*, 1(3): 1-3. https://media.wix.com/ugd/35c673_ c85577fa97964c 7bbbbb8c66304a2499.pdf [Accessed April 10, 2017].

Iyer, A.; Sen, G.; Ostlin, P. (2008). The intersections of gender and class in health status and health care. In Sen, G.; Oslin, P.

(Eds). Gender Inequity in Health: Why It Exists and How We Can Change It, *Global Public Health*, 3(2): Suppl. 1. DOI: http://www.tandfonline.com/doi/full/10.1080/17441690801892174 [Accessed April 10, 2017].

Iyer, A.; Sen, G.; Sreevathsa, A. (2013). Deciphering Rashomon: An approach to verbal autopsies of maternal death. *Global Public Health: An International Journal for Research, Policy and Practice*, 8(4): 389-404. DOI: http://www.tandfonline.com/doi/abs/10.1080/17441692.2013.772219 [Accessed April 10, 2017].

Iyer, A.; Sen, G.; Sreevathsa, A.; Varadan, V. (2012). Verbal autopsies of maternal deaths in Koppal, Karnataka: Lessons from the grave. *BMC Proceedings*, 6(Suppl 1): P2. http://www.biomedcentral.com/1753-6561/6/S1/P2 [Accessed April 10, 2017].

KEMRI-Wellcome Trust Research Programme, Mustang Management Consultants, Ministry of Public Health and Sanitation, Training and Research Support Centre (2011). *Equity Watch 2011: Assessing Progress towards Equity in Health in Kenya*. Nairobi and Harare: KEMRI and EQUINET. http://www.equinetafrica.org/sites/default/files/uploads/documents/Kenya_EW_Dec2011_lfs.pdf [Accessed April 10, 2017].

Kieny, M-P.; Evans, D.; Schmets, G.; Kadandale, S. (2014). Health-system resilience: reflections on the Ebola crisis in western Africa. *Bull World Health Organ*, 92: 850. DOI: http://dx.doi.org/10.2471/BLT.14.149278 [Accessed April 10, 2017].

Knaul, F.M.; Wong, R.; Arreola-Ornelas, H. (2012). Household Spending and Impoverishment. *Financing Health in Latin America Volume 1*. Cambridge, MA: Harvard Global Equity Initiative, in collaboration with Mexican Health Foundation and International Development Research Centre. https://www.idrc.ca/en/book/financing-health-latin-america-household-spending-and-impoverishment [Accessed April 10, 2017].

Kucharski, A.J.; Piot, P. (2014). Containing Ebola virus infection in West Africa. *Euro Surveill.* 2014; 19(36): pii=20899. DOI: http://dx.doi.org/10.2807/1560-7917.ES2014.19.36.20899. http://www.eurosurveillance.org/ViewArticle.aspx?ArticleId=20899 [Accessed April 10, 2017].

Ledogar, R.; Andersson, N. (2002). Social Audits: Fostering Accountability to Local Constituencies. *Capacity.org*, 15, October 22, 2002. http://www.ciet.org/_documents/ 200794114231.pdf [Accessed April 10, 2017].

Lee, K.; Smith, R. (2011). What is 'global health diplomacy'? A conceptual review. *Global Health Governance*, V(I). http://www.ghd-net.org/sites/default/files/Lee-and-Smith_ What-is-Global-Health-Diplomacy_Fall-2011_0.pdf [Accessed April 10, 2017].

Loaiza, E.; Liang, M. (2013). *Adolescent Pregnancy: A Review of the Evidence*. New York: UNFPA. http://www.unfpa.org/sites/default/ files/pub-pdf/ADOLESCENT%20PREGNANCY_UNFPA.pdf [Accessed April 10, 2017].

Loewenson, R.; Laurell, A.C.; Hogstedt, C.; D'Ambruoso, L.; Shroff, Z. (2014). *Participatory action research in health systems: A methods reader.* Harare: TARSC, AHPSR, WHO, International Development Research Centre, EQUINET. http://www.equinetafrica.org/sites/default/files/uploads/ documents/PAR%20Methods%20Reader2014%20for%20web.pdf [Accessed April 10, 2017].

London, L.; Mulumba, M. (2013). Project Title: Health System Governance: Community Participation as a key strategy for realising the Right to Health. Cape Town and Kampala. http://salearningnetwork.weebly.com/uploads/6/5/0/1/6501954/ idrc_first_report_feb_2013.pdf [Accessed April 10, 2017].

Maine, D.; Rosenfield, A. (1999). The Safe Motherhood Initiative: why has it stalled? *American Journal of Public Health*, 89: 480-482.

Maximizing Positive Synergies Academic Consortium (2009). *Interactions between global health initiatives and health systems: Evidence from countries.* June 2009. http://www.who.int/ healthsystems/publications/MPS_academic_case_studies_Book_ 01.pdf [Accessed May 15, 2017].

McIntyre, D.; Mills, A. (2012). Research to support universal coverage reforms in Africa: The SHIELD project. *Health Policy and Planning 2012*, 27(Suppl 1): i1-i3. DOI: https://doi.org/10.1093/ heapol/czs017 [Accessed April 10, 2017].

McIntyre, D.; Kutzin, J. (2016). Health financing country diagnostic: a foundation for national strategy development. Geneva: World Health Organization. http://www.who.int/ health_financing/tools/diagnostic/en/ [Accessed April 10, 2017].

Mhatre, S.; Schryer-Roy, A.-M. (2009). The fallacy of coverage: uncovering disparities to improve immunization rates through evidence. Results from the Canadian International Immunization Initiative Phase 2 – Operational Research Grants. *BMC International Health and Human Rights 2009*, 9(Suppl 1): S1. DOI: 10.1186/1472-698X-9-S1-S1. http://www.biomedcentral.com/ 1472-698X/9/S1/S1 [Accessed April 10, 2017].

Mills A. (2012). Health policy and systems research: defining the terrain; identifying the methods. *Health Policy and Planning*, 27(1): 1-7. DOI: https://doi.org/10.1093/heapol/czr006 [Accessed April 10, 2017].

Mulumba, M. (2016). How the death of two Ugandan mothers is helping entrench the right to health care. *HuffPost.* http://www.huffingtonpost.com/the-conversation-africa/ how-the-death-of-two-ugan_b_9287790.html [Accessed April 10, 2017].

Narasimhan, H.; Boddu, V.; Singh, P.; Katyal, A.; Bergkvist, S.; Rao, M. (2014). The Best Laid Plans: Access to the Rajiv Aarogyasri community health insurance scheme of Andhra Pradesh. *Health,*

Culture and Society, 6(1): 85-97. DOI: 10.5195/hcs.2014.163. http://hcs.pitt.edu [Accessed April 10, 2017].

Odu, B.P.; Mitchell, S.; Isa, H.; Ugot, I.; Yusuf, R.; Cockcroft, A.; Andersson, N. (2015). Equity and seeking treatment for young children with fever in Nigeria: a cross-sectional study in Cross River and Bauchi States. *Infectious Diseases of Poverty*, 3: 1. https://idpjournal.biomedcentral.com/articles/10.1186/2049-9957-4-1; https://www.ncbi.nlm.nih.gov/pmc/articles/PMC4322819/ [Accessed April 10, 2017].

Olivier de Sardan, J.P. (2003). L'enquête socio-anthropologique de terrain : synthèse méthodologique et recommandations à usage des étudiants. *Études et Travaux*, n. 13. http://www.lasdel.net/index.php/nos-activites/etudes-travaux/70-n-13-l-enquete-socioanthropologique-de-terrain-synthese-methodologique-et-recommandations-a-usage-des-etudiants-par-j-p-olivier-de-sardan-2003 [Accessed May 15, 2017].

Olivier de Sardan, J.P. (2015). Health fee exemptions: controversies and misunderstandings around a research programme. Researchers and the public debate. *BMC Health Services Research 2015*, 15(Suppl 3): S4. DOI: 10.1186/1472-6963-15-S3-S4. https://bmchealthservres.biomedcentral.com/articles/10.1186/1472-6963-15-S3-S4 [Accessed April 10, 2017].

Olivier de Sardan, J.P.; Ridde, V. (2015). Public policies and health systems in Sahelian Africa: Theoretical context and empirical specificity. *BMC Health Services Research 2015*, 15(Suppl 3): S3. http://www.biomedcentral.com/1472-6963/15/S3/S3 [Accessed April 10, 2017].

Omer, K.; Afi, N.J.; Baba, M.C.; Adamu, M.; Malami, S.A.; Oyo-Ita, A.; Cockcroft, A.; Andersson, N. (2014). Seeking evidence to support efforts to increase use of antenatal care: a cross-sectional study in two states of Nigeria. *BMC Pregnancy and Childbirth 2014*, 14: 380. http://www.biomedcentral.com/1471-2393/14/380 [Accessed April 10, 2017].

Patton, M.Q. (2011). *Developmental Evaluation: applying complexity concepts to enhance innovation and use.* New York: The Guilford Press.

Planning Commission of India (2011). *High Level Expert Group Report on Universal Health Coverage for India.* New Delhi. http://planningcommission.nic.in/reports/genrep/rep_uhc0812.pdf [Accessed April 10, 2017].

People and research: Improved health systems for West Africans by West Africans (2017). *Health Research Policy and Systems* 15(Suppl 1). https://health-policy-systems-biomedcentral.com/articles/supplements/volume-15-supplement-1 [Accessed July 21, 2017].

Pothapregada, S.; Atun, R. (2009). Interactions between health systems and Global Fund-supported TB and HIV programmes. In: Maximizing Positive Synergies Academic Consortium. *Interactions between global health initiatives and health systems: evidence from countries.* June 2009; pp. 65-73.

Rannan-Eliya, R.P.; Anuranga, C.; Chandrasiri, J.; Hafez, R.; Kasthuri, G.; Wickramasinghe, R.; Jayanthan, J. (2012). *Impact of out-of-pocket expenditures on families and barriers to use of maternal and child health services in Asia and the Pacific: Evidence from national household surveys of healthcare use and expenditures – Summary technical report.* Mandaluyong City, Philippines: Asian Development Bank. https://www.adb.org/sites/default/files/publication/30345/impact-oop-expenditures-mnch-services-asia-pacific.pdf [Accessed April 10, 2017].

Rao M.; Katyal A.; Singh P.V.; Samarth, A.; Bergkvist, S.; Kancharla, M.; Wagstaff, A.; Netuveli, G.; Renton, A. (2014). Changes in addressing inequalities in access to hospital care in Andhra Pradesh and Maharashtra states of India: A difference-in-differences study using repeated cross-sectional surveys. *BMJ Open 2014*: 4:e004471. DOI: 10.1136/bmjopen-2013-004471.

http://bmjopen.bmj.com/content/4/6/e004471.short [Accessed April 10, 2017].

Rosenfield, A.; Maine, D. (1985). Maternal mortality – a neglected tragedy. Where is the 'M' in MCH? *The Lancet*, 326(8446): 83-85.

Save the Children (2015). *A wake-up call: lessons from Ebola for the world's health systems.* London: Save the Children. http://www.savethechildren.org.uk/resources/online-library/wake-call-0 [Accessed April 10, 2017].

Say, L.; Chou, D.; Gemmill, A.; Tunçalp, Ö.; Moller, A-B.; Daniels, J.; (2014). Global Causes of Maternal Death: A WHO Systematic Analysis. *The Lancet Global Health*, 2(6): e323-e333. http://www.thelancet.com/journals/langlo/article/PIIS2214-109X(14)70227-X/fulltext [Accessed April 10, 2017].

Sen, G.; Germain, A.; Chen, L. (1994). *Policies Reconsidered: Health, Empowerment, and Rights.* Boston: Harvard Center for Population and Development Studies.

Sen, G.; Govender, V. (2015). Sexual and reproductive health and rights in changing health systems. *Global Public Health: An International Journal for Research, Policy and Practice*, 10(2): 228-242.

Sen, G.; Iyer, A. (2012). Who gains, who loses and how: Leveraging gender and class intersections to secure health entitlements. *Social Science & Medicine*, 72: 1802-1811. http://www.sciencedirect.com/science/article/pii/S0277953611003236 [Accessed April 10, 2017].

Sen, G.; Iyer, A. (2016). The mechanisms of intersecting social inequalities in health, *BMJ Global Health 2016*, 1(Suppl 1): A35-A36. http://gh.bmj.com/content/1/Suppl_1/A35 [Accessed April 10, 2017].

Sen, G.; Iyer, A.; Mukherjee, C. (2009). A methodology to analyse the intersections of social inequalities in health. *Journal of Human Development and Capabilities*, 10(3): 397-415. DOI: http://www.tandfonline.com/doi/full/10.1080/19452820903048894?scroll=top&needAccess=true [Accessed April 10, 2017].

Sidibé, M. (2016). Universal health coverage: political courage to leave no one behind. *www.thelancet.com/lancetgh*, 4: e355-e356. http://www.thelancet.com/pdfs/journals/langlo/PIIS2214-109X(16)30072-9.pdf [Accessed April 10, 2017].

Singh, S.; Habte, D.; Brown, G. (2010). External review of the Governance Equity and Health Program: Findings brief. Ottawa: IDRC. https://idl-bnc-idrc.dspacedirect.org/handle/10625/47167 [Accessed May 15, 2017].

Thematic Group on Health for All of the Sustainable Development Solutions Network (2014). *Health in the framework of sustainable development: Technical report for the post 2015 development agenda*. Paris and New York: Sustainable Development Solutions Network. http://unsdsn.org/wp-content/uploads/ 2014/02/Health-For-All-Report.pdf [Accessed May 15, 2017].

Training and Research Support Centre and Ministry of Health and Child Care, Zimbabwe (2014). *Zimbabwe Equity Watch 2014: Assessing Progress toward Equity in Health - Zimbabwe*. Harare: TARSC, MoHCC, EQUINET. http://www.equinetafrica.org/sites/default/files/uploads/documents/Zimbabwe_EW_2014.pdf [Accessed April 10, 2017].

UNAIDS (2016). Fact Sheet. November 2016. http://www.unaids.org/sites/default/files/media_asset/UNAIDS_FactSheet_en.pdf [Accessed April 10, 2017].

UNICEF (1987). *Annual report 1987* [Online]. New York: UNICEF. http://www.unicef.org/about/history/files/unicef_annual_report_1987.pdf [Accessed April 10, 2017].

United Nations Population Fund (2004). Programme of Action Adopted at the International Conference on Population and Development, Cairo, 5-13 September 1994: Pocket Edition. http://www.unfpa.org/sites/default/files/event-pdf/PoA_en.pdf [Accessed May 15, 2017].

University of Zambia Department of Economics, Ministry of Health Zambia, TARSC, EQUINET (2011). *Equity Watch 2011: Assessing Progress towards Equity in Health - Zambia*, EQUINET: Lusaka and Harare. http://www.equinetafrica.org/sites/default/files/uploads/documents/Zambia_EW_Aug_2011_web.pdf [Accessed April 10, 2017].

Wigmore, R. (2015). Contextualising Ebola rumours from a political, historical and social perspective to understand people's perceptions of Ebola and the responses to it. Ebola Response Anthropology Platform. http://www.ebola-anthropology.net/key_messages/contextualising-ebola-rumours-from-a-political-historical-and-social-perspective-to-understand-peoples-perceptions-of-ebola-and-the-responses-to-it/ [Accessed April 10, 2017].

Wilkinson, A.; Leach, M. (2014). Briefing: Ebola – Myths, Realities, and Structural Violence. *African Affairs*, 114(454): 136-148. DOI: 10.1093/afraf/adu080. https://academic.oup.com/afraf/article-lookup/doi/10.1093/afraf/adu080 [Accessed April 10, 2017].

Wilson, N. (2015). Safe delivery: How one organization is using the law to improve maternal and child health in Uganda. *Canadian Geographic*. http://idrc.canadiangeographic.ca/blog/improving-maternal-child-care-uganda.asp?platform=hootsuite [Accessed April 10, 2017].

Woog, V.; Singh, S.; Browne, A.; Philbin, J. (2015). Adolescent Women's Need for and Use of Sexual and Reproductive Health Services in Developing Countries. Guttmacher Institute. https://www.guttmacher.org/report/adolescent-womens-need-

and-use-sexual-and-reproductive-health-services-developing-countries [Accessed April 10, 2017].

World Health Organization (1978). Declaration of Alma-Ata. http://www.who.int/publications/almaata_declaration_en.pdf [Accessed April 10, 2017].

World Health Organization (2000). *The World Health Report 2000 - Health systems: Improving performance.* Geneva: WHO. http://www.who.int/whr/2000/en/ [Accessed April 10, 2017].

World Health Organization (2008). *The World Health Report 2008 - Primary Health Care: Now More Than Ever.* Geneva: WHO. http://www.who.int/whr/2008/whr08_en.pdf [Accessed April 10, 2017].

World Health Organization (2010). *The World Health Report 2010 - Health Systems Financing: The Path to Universal Coverage.* Geneva: WHO. http://apps.who.int/iris/bitstream/10665/44371/1/9789241564021_eng.pdf [Accessed April 10, 2017].

World Health Organization (2013). *The World Health Report 2013 - Research for Universal Health Coverage.* Geneva: WHO. http://www.who.int/whr/2013/report/en/ [Accessed April 10, 2017].

World Health Organization (2014). *Making fair choices on the path to universal health coverage: Final report of the WHO Consultative Group on Equity and Universal Health Coverage.* Geneva: WHO. http://www.who.int/choice/documents/making_fair_choices/en/ [Accessed April 10, 2017].

World Health Organization (2016a). *Adolescent pregnancy.* Fact sheet. http://www.who.int/mediacentre/factsheets/fs364/en/ [Accessed April 10, 2017].

World Health Organization (2016b). *Maternal mortality.* Fact sheet. http://www.who.int/mediacentre/factsheets/fs348/en/ [Accessed April 10, 2017].

World Health Organization – Regional Office for Africa (2017). African Health Observatory. Analytical Summary – Health Financing System: Uganda. http://www.aho.afro.who.int/profiles_information/index.php/Uganda:Analytical_summary_Health_financing_system [Accessed April 10, 2017].

World Health Organization and Commission on Social Determinants of Health (2008). *Closing the gap in a generation Health equity through action on the social determinants of health.* Geneva: WHO. http://apps.who.int/iris/bitstream/10665/43943/1/9789241563703_eng.pdf [Accessed April 10, 2017].

World Health Organization, UNICEF, UNFPA, World Bank Group, and United Nations Population Division (2015). *Trends in maternal mortality: 1990 to 2015. Estimates by WHO, UNICEF, UNFPA, World Bank Group and the United Nations Population Division.* http://apps.who.int/iris/bitstream/10665/194254/1/9789241565141_eng.pdf?ua=1 [Accessed April 10, 2017].

Wurie H. (2014). Ebola's collision with the Sierra Leone post-conflict health system, Blog post, Health Systems Global, September 30, 2014. http://healthsystemsglobal.org/blog/14/Ebola-s-collision-with-the-Sierra-Leone-post-conflicthealthsystem.html [Accessed April 10, 2017].

Yamin, A.; Boulanger, V. (2014). Why Global Goals and Indicators Matter: The Experience of Sexual and Reproductive Health and Rights in the Millennium Development Goals. *Journal of Human Development and Capabilities*, 15(2-3): 218-231.

Zikusooka, C.M.; Loewenson, R.; Tumwine, M.; Mulumba, M. (2010). *Equity Watch 2011: Assessing progress towards equity in health – Uganda.* Kampala and Harare: EQUINET. http://www.equinet africa.org/sites/default/files/uploads/documents/Uganda_EW_Nov2011_lfs.pdf [Accessed April 10, 2017].

The Publisher

Canada's International Development Research Centre (IDRC) funds practical research in developing countries to increase prosperity and security, and to foster democracy and the rule of law, in support of Canada's international development efforts. We promote growth and development and encourage sharing knowledge with policymakers, other researchers, and communities around the world. The result is innovative, lasting solutions that aim to bring change to those who need it most.

IDRC Books publishes research results and scholarly studies on global and regional issues related to sustainable and equitable development. As a specialist in development literature, IDRC Books contributes to the body of knowledge on these issues to further the cause of global understanding and equity. The full catalogue is available at **www.idrc.ca**.